The
Authenticity
Principle

Resist Conformity,
Embrace Differences,
and Transform
How You Live,
Work, and Lead

The
Authenticity
Principle

Ritu Bhasin

MELANIN MADE PRESS

Melanin Made Press
Toronto ON

Cataloguing data available from Library and Archives Canada
ISBN 978-1-7750162-0-5 (paperback)
ISBN 978-1-7750162-1-2 (ebook)

Produced by Page Two
www.pagetwostrategies.com
Cover and interior design by Peter Cocking
Cover photo by Calvin Thomas

17 18 19 20 21   5 4 3 2 1

www.bhasinconsulting.com

To inquire about bulk purchases,
contact info@bhasinconsulting.com

For my "angels."

Thank you for embracing who I am,
encasing me with your love,
helping me to shine,
and letting me do the same for you.

When she transformed into a butterfly, the caterpillars spoke not of her beauty, but of her weirdness. They wanted her to change back into what she always had been. But she had wings.

DEAN JACKSON

Contents

Introduction

Those who hear not the music think the dancers mad.

UNKNOWN

I RECALL THE first time I was made to feel inferior because
I was different from the people around me. I was about five
years old and playing with a small group of White girls. We
were playing "tea time" with my tea set—picture a Royal Doulton-
type white-and-blue flowered plastic tea set. One of the girls
asked me why one side of my hands was white and the other side
was brown. As the only little Brown girl in the group, I looked
down at my hands and said, "I don't know."

I remember the girls telling me that because only one side
was white, because I wasn't like them, they were going to put
dirt into my cup and they wanted me to drink dirt-water as tea.
So I did. Out of *my own* tea set.

This is just the first in a long string of memories that I have
from my childhood and teenage years of being bombarded with
messages that something was wrong with me—that I was "less
than"—because of what made me different.

I was born in Toronto to parents who immigrated to Canada
in the early 1970s from India, leaving behind their upper-class
lifestyle to start at the bottom in a new country. As practicing
Sikhs, my father wears a turban to cover his unshorn hair, and

my mother also has long, uncut hair. My parents chose to raise my siblings and me in an affluent, primarily White suburb. It was a financial stretch for them, but they wanted us to flourish and they believed that, as Canadian-born Brown kids growing up with wealthier White kids, we'd have access to better education, build better networks, and move up the social ladder.

Our parents wanted us to be part of both Punjabi and Canadian culture, and they raised us with a strict code around the "right" ways of speaking, emoting, dressing, eating, addressing conflict, and more. It was a challenging, nuanced, and confusing code to adhere to. I often felt caught in a mishmash of cultural identities—Punjabi/Sikh, British-influenced Indian, and Canadian—and my naturally gregarious, energetic, and feisty ways didn't mesh particularly well with any of these cultures.

Growing up as one of a few children of color in a homogeneous suburb, I also struggled with my identity among my peers. I felt different because I *was* different: I had a long black braid that reached well past my waist. My clothes were clean and neat but weren't the designer brands the "rich kids" wore. I was stick-thin and had a unibrow, hairy arms and legs, an overbite, thick glasses, and acne. I brought chicken curry and basmati rice to school for lunch, not the fake cheese dip that came with crackers and a red stick that my peers ate and I coveted. I wasn't allowed to do the things my White peers did, like go on sleepovers and hang out with boys. And, to top it off, I excelled in academics and was often the teacher's pet.

I was relentlessly bullied by my peers and supposed friends. I experienced the "I Hate Ritu" club, "Ritu, the Curry Queen" drawings, comments about my "towel-rag-wearing" father, and incessant questions about why my clothes/shoes/house/car weren't nicer, not to mention the non-stop racist insults, teasing, and harassment. It wasn't just that I felt different; it was that *because* of my differences, I was made to feel unwanted, unworthy, and unlovable.

I internalized the hostility and racism I experienced, and I started to believe that there was something wrong with being Brown. I desperately wanted to "fit in" and so, during my high school years, I convinced my parents to let me cut my hair to shoulder-length, and at times I even had it dyed a frightening orange-ish. I alternated between wearing green and blue contact lenses, almost changed my name to a "White name" (this book would have been written by Carise Bhasin), and got a job at a fashionable clothing store, which dramatically upped my wardrobe and image. I also got braces, cleared up the acne, shed the body fur, and filled out. When invited by friends, I went to cottages (lovely), tried to learn how to golf (boring) and to ski (dangerous), and watched so much hockey my eyes hurt (never again). I had multiple crushes on White boys and when one finally liked me, I dated him for years even though I was unhappy, worried that it would be hard to find someone else to date me. In all of these ways I was *performing* and, in doing so, I was attempting to signal to my peers that I may not be affluent or White but that I could try to act it.

In using the term "performing," I mean the negative or harmful sense of the word: acting in a way that we wish we didn't have to and that feels disempowering. As children, most of us are taught to create a Performing Self—a self that alters, masks, cloaks, and minimizes our behavioral preferences, desires, spirit, and differences in order to be accepted by our loved ones, peers, colleagues, and society as a whole. But performing is an unfulfilling and unhealthy way of living. When we unwillingly change our behavior based on what others think about or expect from us, we give away our power, because others then control our happiness.

The more I performed by showing up the way my parents and peers wanted me to, the more I was incentivized to do so because in return I perceived that I was receiving love, validation, and a sense of belonging. I also came to see that when I stepped outside of expected behaviors, not only would I be judged by others, but this love, validation, and sense of belonging could be taken away. I consistently received messages to alter and mask my behavioral preferences and I lived in constant fear that I would be found out. So, while I became a master at conforming and masking, I was unhappy. I desperately wanted to march to the beat of my own drum, but instead I was both confused about and hiding my true self—my Authentic Self.

As adults, we are projections of what we've experienced as children. If we grew up internalizing that there's something wrong with us or that we need to conform or mask who we are in order to receive love and acceptance, when we're older, the adverse effects will show up in how we live, love, play, work, and lead. Worn out from the unhealthy messages and ways of being that we've internalized, some of us will eventually choose to do self-work so that we can be happier, healthier, and more tapped into our potential. This self-work forms the basis of what I call the Authenticity Principle: a framework for resisting conformity, embracing differences, and transforming our lives.

I continued to perform by masking many aspects of who I am, well into my adulthood before I realized how lost I was. I navigated law school and the legal profession (a homogeneous and conforming world) for over ten years by curating an image of being happy as a lawyer and then as a director at a law firm—"I am flawless, I am so confident, I am just like you"—which I used to hide my fears about being an outsider and to shield against judgments. My Performing Self also showed up constantly in my friendships and romantic relationships, pushing me further away from how I really wanted to live.

On the surface, things may have seemed peachy—I was successful, well-liked by my colleagues, and socially integrated within elite circles, with lots of friends and romantic interests. But I was hurting inside. I felt spiritually vacant, disconnected from myself, deflated about my differences, and exhausted from performing. As an adult responsible for her own happiness, I was aching for a better sense of who I really was and for the ability and confidence to radiate it.

As I'll share throughout the book, a confluence of experiences ten years ago pushed me to make a commitment to be honest *with* myself *about* myself, which then led to a series of positive life changes: I made the decision to leave the legal profession and the world of being an employee to start my own leadership and inclusion consulting practice, which I love. I shed relationships that weren't serving me any longer and I developed new ones with people who know me and love me for who I really am. I drew boundaries and started to speak my truth more openly with family members, accepting the negative consequences even when painful.

But the most important decision I made was to embrace the Authenticity Principle—it truly transformed my life. Through my self-work, I discovered that I could *choose* to live, work, and lead more authentically and change my life in a positive, powerful way. By choosing to understand myself better and be more of who I am, I felt more elevated, confident, and creative. And I found that the better I felt about myself, the more I was able to share who I am with others, which led others to do the same with me.

Living authentically gave me the wings to take flight in all aspects of my life, and my goal with this book is to share my insights so that you, too, can achieve this. I want you to feel beautiful in your skin because you shouldn't have to feel any other way. Full stop.

The Transformative Power of Authenticity

As a leadership, inclusion, and mindfulness professional, I'm passionate about empowerment, social justice, and mental/

physical/spiritual well-being for all. My mission is to create a more empowered and inclusive world, and I work at doing this by teaching people how to be more culturally competent, emotionally intelligent, mindful, and authentic.

My work in the areas of diversity and inclusion, in particular, have been a tremendous force in saving me from a life of performing. As I dug deeper and deeper into exploring how discomfort with differences is entrenched in our culture, I came to learn about the tremendous societal pressure many of us feel to conform and mask who we are and the detrimental impact of the negative messaging we receive on our ability to love ourselves ("self-love"). This helped me to better understand how I was rejecting my Authentic Self, and especially the fundamental aspects of myself that make me unique and different.

Through my work, I've learned that I'm not alone: so many of us feel lost, confused, and caught up in the pressure to project a "curated life"—one where we signal to the world that we're more joyful, more in love, and more successful than we actually are. We feel the need to mask our vulnerabilities and pain, in the hopes that the "I'm so happy" image we've constructed will provide us with cover. But, in truth, we're drained from pretending. We also hurt because, in a world that pushes us to conform and where intolerance swirls around us, we fear judgment and rejection. In turn, we often internalize the negative messages that come our way about who we are, and we minimize and mask aspects of our identities. We do this with ourselves, in our relationships, in our social interactions, and, in our adult lives, probably most of all at work.

For example, through my consulting and speaking engagements, my research, and my coaching work, I've now had hundreds of women, people of color, people from LGBT communities, persons with disabilities, and others share with me the impact they've felt as a result of oppression and xenophobia, and how they alter, downplay, and hide their cultural differences (such as not telling others that they're Muslim, passing as straight or cisgender, or hiding painful diseases). People have revealed to me their feelings of anger about being marginalized as well as feelings of woundedness, unworthiness, shame, and not belonging. And they've disclosed how internalizing the biases and hate coming their way has caused them to self-loathe and become unsure of who they are and what it means to express themselves authentically. I empathize with these experiences because this has been my story too.

While I've learned about the harm caused by judgment and conformity, more importantly, I've learned about the transformative power of authenticity in healing the wounds that come from feeling we're unlovable because of our differences. I've come to see how embracing our differences and behaving in ways that reflect who we really are can help us to feel more connected, centered, empowered, confident, and creative. Authenticity is the antidote to exclusion—whether it be in relationships, social interactions, or the workplace—because, at its core, inclusion is about encouraging each of us to be who we truly are as much as possible. Ultimately, authenticity creates joy.

In writing this book, I had the privilege of spending over eighty hours interviewing fifty-five people from around the world—leaders, entrepreneurs, artists, and change agents from a range of backgrounds. Regardless of which discipline they're in or what role they play, they all shine at what they do. Every single person I spoke with said the same thing: their lives are enhanced because they choose to be their Authentic Self in as many moments as possible. They are happy because they embrace what makes them different. They also recognize that being authentic can sometimes have negative consequences, based on how others perceive them. But despite these potential downsides, they choose to be authentic anyway. What each and every person I interviewed told me is that it hurts to be someone they're not—whether it is with themselves, at home with their loved ones, at work, or when they're out and about in the world. Conversely, they said they find that living authentically gives them clarity, meaning, and purpose in how they live, work, and lead.

Che Kothari, artist and self-described instigator, beautifully articulated to me how being authentic is the first step in a chain reaction that will result in you becoming a happier version of yourself. He described the domino effect of pursuing authenticity: authenticity is rooted in an understanding of the self, and self-understanding leads to self-respect; in turn, self-respect leads to self-trust, self-trust leads to self-love, self-love leads to unconditional love—and unconditional love of the self is your ultimate goal for achieving self-actualization.

In other words, practicing authenticity is the catalyst to realizing your full potential—and this is the foundation of the Authenticity Principle. It's a disruptive and comprehensive way for living, working, and leading more as who you really are.

Step into Your Life with the Authenticity Principle

In this book, I will reveal to you why and how embracing the Authenticity Principle will be instrumental in making you happier and more confident as a person; more loving as a spouse, parent, and friend; more successful as a professional; more effective as a leader; more creative and innovative as a team member; and more inclusive as a member of society. You'll learn that the Authenticity Principle is rooted in the concept that when we consistently choose to know, embrace, and be who we are—especially our differences—as often as possible, we feel better about ourselves, we bring this spirit to our interactions, and, in so doing, we invite others to do the same. As a result, not only do we feel more connected to ourselves, we build more meaningful relationships with others.

As I'll discuss in further detail in the chapters that follow, the Authenticity Principle leverages a continuum I've developed called the Three Selves, which is a more nuanced way of understanding authentic behavior—the idea that rather than being either "authentic" or "inauthentic," each of us possesses the following three selves:

- **Authentic Self:** If there were no negative consequences for your actions, your Authentic Self is who you would be.

- **Adapted Self:** When you willingly choose to adapt your Authentic Self's behavior in order to meet your needs and others' needs, you reveal your Adapted Self.

- **Performing Self:** When you feel you don't have a choice but to conform or mask who you are, your Performing Self is who you show up as.

Using the Three Selves continuum, I will show you how the objective of the Authenticity Principle is to push away from being your Performing Self (which feels disempowering, as you'll have seen from my story and you'll have experienced yourself) and instead flow between being your Adapted Self (which feels good) and your Authentic Self (which feels the most empowering). At its core, the Authenticity Principle is about the power of *choice* in how you live. It's about how you *choose* to be your Authentic Self and your Adapted Self as much as possible by knowing who you are, embracing who you are, and then being who you are. You'll see that authenticity is a practice—your choices move you closer to or further from your true self. The focus is on *you* and *your* actions.

This book isn't intended as a "how-to" for developing your radar to determine how authentic others are (although I suspect that after reading this book you'll be able to better discern this).

This book is focused on teaching you to leverage the Authenticity Principle—to determine what living, working, and leading authentically mean for you—through strategies rooted in leadership, neuroscience, inclusion, and mindfulness. To that end, in some of the chapters you'll see short sections entitled "Reflection Moments," consisting of a few questions that will encourage you to pause for a moment, engage in self-inquiry, and capture your thoughts (which I recommend doing by either writing them down in the book or in a journal, or typing them out, as brain science tells us that this is more effective for behavioral change than just contemplating the responses in your head).

In chapter 1, we'll explore what authenticity is, including an overview of the Three Selves continuum. In chapters 2 and 3, we'll do a deep dive into exploring the Authentic Self. In chapters 4 to 7, we'll explore the Performing Self in depth by examining the barriers that get in the way of authenticity, especially within the workplace—the domain where we're most likely to perform as adults—and how to better embrace who we are. In chapters 8 and 9, we'll explore the Adapted Self and how you can learn to be adaptive in moments that call for it. And finally, in chapter 10, we'll examine authentic leadership and how we can foster a culture of authenticity and inclusion in our interactions with others. Many leaders speak of the importance of enabling their team members to bring their whole selves to work—this chapter sets out how to make that happen.

As you dig into the book, my hope is that you'll start to practice living in alignment with the Authenticity Principle immediately—that you'll ditch the need for perfection, the right moment, or whatever it is that's stopping you, and you'll just start now.

The message "start now" is something I have learned from my rock star sister, Komal. By day Komal is a mental health care executive and advocate, and by night she teaches meditation and yoga. One of the inspirations for her teaching is a conversation she had with a Tibetan taxi driver during a ride years ago about *gom*, the Tibetan word for meditation. He taught Komal that there is no perfect way of meditating; you should just start in whatever form you can. Meditate now—every moment can be meditative if you are present and aware.

In the same way, you can start the practice of being yourself this very minute. Commit to being more authentic as you start to turn these pages. Take a deep breath and leap.

1

A New Way of Understanding Authenticity

You're born naked and the rest is drag.

RUPAUL

MANY YEARS ago, I was at the Calgary airport flying back from a work engagement. Before heading to my gate, I decided to stop at the nearest coffee shop. When I got to the front of the line, I noticed that the three brown-skinned women behind the counter were speaking Punjabi to each other (my parents' first language and my second). My natural inclination when I hear people speaking Punjabi is to join in, so as I approached the counter, the words were about to roll off my tongue when I heard the voice in my head say, "No, speak English." I felt my body stiffen and then proceeded to order using the Queen's English.

I knew as soon as it happened that I had self-censored. I wasn't sure why, but I knew that it didn't feel right. As I waited for my order, I reflected on what had just transpired, and I gave myself a pep talk. Despite my discomfort, I told myself: "Be real. Say it in Punjabi!" So when my Punjabi "sista" asked me in English what I wanted in my tuna wrap, I responded in the loudest and most expressive Punjabi I could muster.

Of course, I startled the hell out of the poor thing. Her eyes widened at first, but then she got it together and did what most people do when they're on the receiving end of a vibrant greeting—she smiled and started to chat with me. In Punjabi. And then the other women turned around and smiled too. When I left, our parting words were in Punjabi, but more importantly, we gave each other the warm "I got you" look that people share when they have a chance to connect with others from the same culture, especially in environments where that doesn't happen often.

This was a pivotal moment for me. For one, I had consciously caught myself holding back an essential cultural aspect of who I am, and it made me realize that if I was doing it for the Punjabi language at an airport coffee shop over a tuna wrap, then it was undoubtedly happening in other moments of my life—and likely moments that were far more crucial to my personal and professional happiness and success.

Through my self-work over time, I came to understand why my initial reaction that day was to hold back from being authentic: I was standing in the long coffee shop line with mostly White men in fancy business suits. Because I had learned to downplay my cultural differences in order to "fit in" with White people, my brain was thinking that if I spoke in Punjabi, it would have highlighted that I was different and, more specifically, "less than" the White men who were in the line. I wanted to shield against judgment so that I would feel safe and, in doing so, I stopped myself from being true to my Authentic Self.

Initially it was hard for me to acknowledge that I was carrying negative messaging about my differences into my adulthood. But I knew that in order to live more authentically, I needed to identify how the tendencies to conform and mask who I am were showing up in my behavior.

Loaded moments like these are powerful lessons in our journey of practicing authenticity because they reveal to us how we're conforming and masking to "fit in." They also reveal to us how we actually want to behave and, with this knowledge in hand, we can work to make this happen going forward.

To help you recognize what being authentic looks and feels like for you, we'll start by exploring what is meant by "authenticity."

What Is Authenticity?

Authenticity is a hot topic right now. We hear about it constantly in relation to leadership, management, entrepreneurship, psychotherapy, spirituality, mindfulness, well-being, romance, and parenting. While we may hear from time to time that authenticity is overrated and misguided, the overwhelming consensus seems to be that it is critical for happiness and empowerment,[1] which is felt in all areas of life, as follows:

- **Being authentic creates personal joy:** In the research and writings on how to live a happy life (i.e., find personal joy), so much ties back to knowing, embracing, and being who we are at our core. Being authentic is directly connected with how we find meaning and live out our purpose in life, and so it's a key ingredient in the mix that impacts our self-esteem, our self-confidence, our feelings of being included or excluded, our feelings of autonomy, our psychological functioning and well-being, and our mental and physical health.[2]

- **Being authentic creates relational joy:** When we're authentic in our interactions with others, we're more likely to create space for others to do the same with us, thereby allowing us to build more meaningful and lasting connections. And not surprisingly, research shows that having strong, high-quality relationships is crucial for living a happy and fulfilled life.[3]

This is significant for our capacity as leaders—which we all are in some form because we all motivate, inspire, incentivize, and direct others to follow us in some way (think of your role as a lover, parent, friend, teacher, boss, mentor or sponsor, coach, etc.)—because by being authentic, we help to create more empowered, engaged, and inclusive relationships, environments, and organizations. If that's not reason enough, being authentic also impacts who we attract into our lives.

- **Being authentic creates professional joy:** Research shows that happier employees are more productive at work.[4] And, of course, happiness impacts our morale at work, our quality of work, our ability to be creative and innovative, our team interactions, our desire to advance, and whether we leave our job or stay. Part of what influences whether we're happy at work is the extent to which we feel comfortable being authentic with our leaders and team members.

I interviewed Bruce Croxon, an entrepreneur (he was a co-founder of Lavalife, the pioneering online dating site) and television personality, for this book. Bruce personifies authenticity: he is self-aware, gets vulnerable, and speaks his truth even when uncomfortable. Bruce attributes his professional success to living authentically, as opposed to attributing his authenticity to his success. He explained that, well before his success, he focused on building incredible relationships: "I had nothing, but I was building real relationships with people everywhere I went, through authenticity. Now my ability to do this leads to better business relationships—and partnerships have been the key to my business success. I didn't expect this back then, but learning to be authentic has been a huge payoff."

Authentic Living Insight
Connecting Authenticity and Entrepreneurship

If you're teetering on the edge of wanting to launch your own business, having the freedom to be more authentic is another motivation to do it.

In my interview with business columnist Leah Eichler, she told me about how, after years of railing against conformity in a corporate culture, she left to start her own business and found that it enabled her to be more of herself. And true to her word, on the day of our interview, Leah was sporting streaks of electric blue color in her otherwise blond hair.

Interestingly, every entrepreneur I interviewed told me the same thing about their experiences with practicing authenticity: because the organizational values they're tied to are their own and they largely have personal and professional autonomy, they naturally feel freer to be authentic.

On a personal note, I too have found that running my own business enables me to be more of my Authentic Self at work because, as the leader, I create my firm's cultural norms, rather than follow others' norms. And with this freedom to be more authentic, I feel more inspired, creative, and innovative than I ever have before. In other words, I'm better at my job because I get to be, and am, more authentic.

While the benefits of living authentically are clear, what's less clear in the current dialogue is what exactly authenticity *is* and how we do it. The advice to "be yourself" feels meaningless without a more in-depth understanding of the concept. So our starting point is getting to the root of what is meant by "authenticity" in the context of how we live, work, and lead.

The word "authentic" originates from the Latin *authenticus* and the Greek *authentikos*, meaning "genuine or original." And this is generally how most dictionaries define authenticity. While I agree that authenticity connects with being genuine, in my view being authentic is about better understanding and being who we truly are, which may or may not be tied back to being original, unique, or different.

I define authenticity as the practice of consistently choosing to know, embrace, and be who we are as often as possible. It requires that we have a solid understanding of our Authentic Self and Adapted Self, that we accept who we really are by cultivating self-love, and that we exercise the choice to behave as our Authentic Self and Adapted Self as often as possible with ourselves and with others. The Authenticity Principle builds on this definition, focusing on the power of choice—deciding to be ourselves even in the face of judgment and other negative consequences.

Here's a key insight: authenticity isn't a permanent or constant state of being. No one can be authentic 100 percent of the time. It's unrealistic and unattainable for a number of reasons, including the need to conform to certain societal, cultural, familial, and organizational norms. Instead, an authentic life consists of multiple moments in which we consistently *choose* to be ourselves. Many of us hope that if we do ABC today, then tomorrow we will have arrived at "Authenticity," but this, unfortunately, is not how it works. In fact, most of the people I interviewed didn't tell me they are authentic in every single thing they do but that they *try* to be authentic as much as possible in their choices and behaviors. In this way, they live in alignment with the Authenticity Principle.

For example, in my upbringing, I was taught to stifle dissent and to hide my flaws. I was encouraged to focus on projecting pleasant agreement and perfection. As part of this conditioning, I also learned to suppress anger and sadness ("bad" emotions) and instead to project happiness as much as possible ("good" emotions). The accepted behaviors were smiling, saying "Everything is great!" and acting like sunshine (which also happens to be one of my nicknames), even if I felt like shit. I often felt that I had to alter how I wanted to behave in order to meet others' behavioral expectations. I often couldn't be myself or embrace myself, which was not only very confusing but also made it harder for me to understand who my Authentic Self actually was. Because of this deep internal disconnect, I sometimes felt "fake," and I now know from the feedback I've received from work friends from my days in the legal profession that they thought I was being fake too. I was living a paradox: in trying not to feel any of the emotions I perceived of as bad, I was actually blocking my path to experiencing joy in all areas of my life. It resulted in heaps of internalized gunk—in other words, pain and suffering.

But now, with my commitment to practicing authenticity as a way of life, I try as much as possible to *choose* to be my true self in as many moments as possible, which means that I increasingly invite myself to sit in the truth of how I feel. If that means crying, I cry. If I want to rant, I rant. Of course, there are times when the "bad" emotions arise, and I want to quickly push them away. But I try to resist the temptation to do that and instead focus on *choosing* to be true to them, which means expressing the feelings. Most importantly, I now don't feel as much pressure to be smiley, shiny, and happy when I'm not feeling that way. Funnily enough, allowing myself to feel bad when I actually do has made me feel happier overall. And even though it sometimes seems hard for people who are used to "Sunshine Ritu" to adjust to, I do it anyway—because I feel better being me than performing a role.

You, too, can learn to make choices about how to reveal more of yourself by leveraging the continuum I call the Three Selves.

The Three Selves

Our society seems to have a very binary way of looking at authenticity: you're either behaving authentically or you're not, in which case you're being "inauthentic." Not only do I disagree with using this terminology (see the sidebar below for why that is), but my work has revealed that this binary lens oversimplifies human behavior and doesn't take into account the power of choice in how we live. Authenticity isn't a switch you automatically flick from "on" to "off," but rather it's a series of decisions we make for and about ourselves, again and again.

Authentic Living Insight
Why Not Use the Term "Inauthenticity"?

I very deliberately have chosen not to use the words "inauthentic" and "inauthenticity" in my work.

When most of us veer from being authentic, either we don't want to do it or we don't know we're doing it. Oftentimes, the fear we harbor about the potential negative consequences of being authentic, or our previous hurtful experiences of being judged, gives rise to feelings of vulnerability, which in turn reinforces the learned behavior of conforming or masking—a self-defense mechanism to protect us from the pain we fear will come from being authentic. We aren't actively choosing to deceive or mislead when we're not being our true selves, which is what the harshness of the word "inauthentic" often implies.

I recently presented to a group of leaders on the power of authenticity and, in the midst of my talk, a trans woman audience member courageously shared a bit about her journey with living authentically. She disclosed that, while she had transitioned years prior, she still finds it hard at times to self-identify and to talk about her experiences as a transgender person. She emphasized that when she chooses not to reveal or talk about her identity in certain moments, it's not because she's being "inauthentic"; it's because she fears judgment and for her safety. It was a powerful learning moment.

To call someone "inauthentic" without understanding the depth of their feelings of fear, pain, vulnerability, imperfection, unworthiness, and shame is a missed opportunity to practice empathy. We need to offer others the same kindness and compassion we give to ourselves in our own journey of identifying and addressing the barriers to living authentically.

For example, Sean Tompkins, who's the CEO of a UK-headquartered global real estate and construction organization, told me in our interview that he's committed to being authentic and then he added: "Sometimes I adapt because being authentic isn't good for my kids or my team—it's not what they need in the moment, and I'm fine to change my behavior to give them what they need." Would this mean that Sean, and every one of us who willingly alters our behavior, is not being authentic? I don't feel this is right.

The Three Selves concept will allow you to better understand how you can adjust your behavior based on how much of your Authentic Self you feel comfortable sharing in any given moment. It reflects a continuum of three primary experiences when it comes to behaving authentically, as follows:

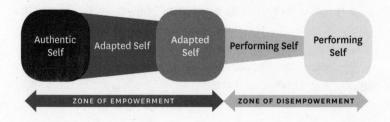

- **Your Authentic Self:** Who you would choose to be if there were no consequences for your actions. This self reflects the fusion of your core values, beliefs, needs, desires, thoughts, emotions, and traits—and how you would behave if you didn't live in fear of the consequences. In moments when you're being your Authentic Self, you experience alignment in how you're thinking, feeling, and behaving. The more you can be your Authentic Self, the more you'll cultivate personal, relational, and professional joy—ultimately, the more you will feel empowered. Some of us spend only a bit of our time here.

- **Your Adapted Self:** Who you are when you willingly *choose* to alter your behavior from how your Authentic Self would act. The Adapted Self is a critical place along the authenticity continuum, because you're exercising choice to adapt your behavior in order to serve your own needs and others' needs (for example, you need to make friends, keep your job, not go to jail). You're still being you as your Adapted Self, and because you're exercising choice to do so, you feel satisfied to be in this state (unlike when you're being your Performing Self). The key point is that you see the benefit of choosing to be adaptive, which is why you do it, so you're still being true to yourself. In adapting your behavior, you're in service of authenticity because you're choosing to fulfill your authentic needs or desires in that particular moment. As your Adapted Self, you feel aligned and empowered. Some of us spend much of our time here.

- **Your Performing Self:** Who you show up as when you feel like you can't be yourself and don't have a choice but to conform or mask who you really are, and it feels bad. This is the curated life you put out there. It's the constructed persona that you project—both knowingly and unknowingly—by conforming or masking who you are in order to protect against what you perceive would be the negative consequences of being yourself. For example, you feel like you can't share your opinion, disagree with anyone, wear what you want, or express your sadness because, if you do, others will take their love away, be less likely to work with you, or stop spending time with you. It's the self that causes you to feel the most disconnected, unfulfilled, and powerless because *fear* removes your ability to be who you truly are. As your Performing Self, you feel misaligned and disempowered. Some of us spend a lot of time here.

Your Authentic Self

Description	Key Attributes	How It Feels
Who you would be if there were no negative consequences for your actions	• A reflection of your core values, beliefs, needs, desires, thoughts, emotions, and traits	• Empowering
		• Like alignment
		• Fulfilling
	• You have alignment in how you're thinking, feeling, and behaving	• Liberating
	• You feel belonging in your interactions with others	

Your Adapted Self

Description	Key Attributes	How It Feels
Who you are when you willingly choose to alter your behavior from how your Authentic Self would act, to meet your needs and others' needs	• You feel like you have the *choice* to alter your behavior from how your Authentic Self would behave, and you do so willingly	• Empowering
		• Like alignment
		• Satisfying
		• Strategic
	• Still a reflection of your values, beliefs, needs, desires, thoughts, emotions, and traits	
	• You feel belonging in your interactions with others	

Your Performing Self

Description	Key Attributes	How It Feels
Who you show up as when you feel you don't have a choice but to conform or mask who you are	• You feel like you lack choice on how to behave • Fear takes away your ability to be who you truly are • You conform—alter your behavior to "fit in" • You mask—hide aspects of who you are • Cultivates feelings of "fitting in" in your interactions with others, but not belonging	• Disempowering • Like misalignment • Disconnecting • Unfulfilling • Exclusionary • Hurtful • Threatening • Exhausting

Here's where the Three Selves continuum gets even more interesting and nuanced. We're not consistently one of our Three Selves in every moment; rather, in any given moment, how we behave may reflect that in some ways we're being authentic, in some ways we're being adaptive, and in some ways we're performing.

We become aware of the extent to which we're being authentic, or to which we're performing, by understanding how we're acting in what I call the "Seven Behavioral Dimensions." (We're going to keep coming back to the dimensions, so I encourage you to become very familiar with them.) Created based on my work, the Seven Behavioral Dimensions reflect a range of behaviors in which we make decisions about how to act at any time.

All day long, we're knowingly and unknowingly making decisions about how to behave in the following seven key areas:

- **How we express our emotions:** This dimension reflects the extent to which we are restrained or expressive in how we express ourselves across a range of emotions: anger, fear, disgust, happiness, sadness, surprise, contempt, shame, and pride.[5]

- **How we communicate non-verbally:** This dimension covers how we behave in areas like gesturing, touching, posture, facial expressions, eye contact, and what I call "eye talk" (blinking, squinting, widening, closing, rolling, "smizing," glaring, etc.).

- **The words we use when we speak:** This dimension includes whether we speak formally or informally; what vocabulary we choose (e.g., using simple words as opposed to bigger, fancier, less commonly used words); whether we use slang, swear words, or offensive language.

- **How we speak:** This dimension reflects the pitch, volume, pace, accent, and intonation of our voice.

- **Our appearance:** This dimension reflects how we choose to physically present ourselves, including our clothing, shoes, makeup, hairstyle, weight, cosmetic procedures/plastic surgery, jewelry, piercings, tattoos, accessories, style, brand affiliation, and the colors we wear.

- **The content we share:** This dimension includes what we put forward about our values, beliefs, thoughts, ideas, opinions, dissenting views, stories, experiences, and cultural differences—which, broadly defined, includes our nationality, race/ethnoculture, religion/faith, gender identity, sexual orientation, age, disability, class/socioeconomic status, and family status.

- **Our actions:** This dimension covers the countless decisions we make every day about how we act, including the choices we make about how to treat people, whom to speak to, whom to avoid, how we self-promote, whose interests we prioritize, how and whom we defer to, how and whom we dominate, how we listen, what we say yes/no/maybe to, and how and where we draw our boundaries.

As you learn to leverage the Seven Behavioral Dimensions in being more authentic, you'll come to see that in any given moment, you may choose to be authentic in some of the dimensions but choose to adapt your behavior in other dimensions. You may also feel pushed to perform in some of them. To live more authentically, it's essential that you develop a comprehensive understanding of your preferred way of behaving across these dimensions and how you're actually behaving. This understanding will illuminate not only what being authentic looks like for you, it will also reveal in what ways you're conforming or masking to fit in.

For example, at a team meeting you may *choose to be authentic* with your posture, your hand gestures, and your facial expressions and with how you use your voice. You may *choose to adapt* your behaviors by using more formal language when you speak and by holding back on demonstrating your disagreement with the decisions being made. And you may *be pushed to perform* by hiding that the real reason you're being quiet at the meeting is because you're afraid you'll be judged if you share that you're not feeling well today because of depression. In this example, then, you'd be showing up in the meeting in part as your Authentic Self, in part as your Adapted Self, and in part as your Performing Self. Your behavioral choices would reflect that your authentic state falls across the Three Selves continuum.

The ideal situation, of course, is to make choices that reflect your Authentic Self and your Adapted Self as much as possible in each of the behavioral dimensions, so that you're in what I call the "zone of empowerment," with very few, if any, moments of being your Performing Self. The more you find yourself in a place where you're pushed to perform in several of the behavioral dimensions, the more you'll feel misaligned and disempowered.

In our second interview about living and leading authentically, Drew Dudley and I met at a restaurant in Toronto. Drew is a global leadership speaker who many will know from his extremely popular TED Talk on "lollipop leadership," which reminds people that they have the capacity to matter each day. I had ordered a green tea, and in our conversation about flowing between being your Authentic Self and your Adapted Self, Drew reached over, took hold of the teapot, and used it to make a great analogy to describe the experience of being authentic versus being adaptive versus performing: "Choosing how authentic you want to be in a situation is still being authentic. It's like pouring water out of this teapot. Let's pretend this teapot is your Authentic Self, who you are. How much water you pour out of this teapot is up to you—but as long as you're pouring out of this teapot and not another one, you're still being you." This analogy perfectly captures the experience of being authentic versus being adaptive—with your Adapted Self, you're still choosing to pour out of the same teapot of who you are; whereas with your Performing Self, you'd be reaching for an entirely new teapot that is not who you are. As Drew put it, "When you start to act like someone you're not, that's not authentic. You're not pouring from the same teapot."

Authentic Living Insight
The Green–Yellow–Red Light Self-Assessment Test

In my discussion with Tim Thompson, who's a chief operating officer of a division of a global bank, he spoke of his journey of learning to be more open about being gay. It was the "big markers in life" that pushed Tim to want to live more authentically—his experiences with coming out of the closet, finding out he had prostate cancer, and adopting children through surrogacy. "Being authentic is about taking incremental steps of practicing authenticity," he told me. "You open the door and take a step, and then another step, and another step, until you feel you've climbed a level. And then you open another door."

Despite how far he's come in his journey, Tim spoke very openly about the sting of being made to feel like something is wrong with him because he's gay: "Sometimes you feel threatened as a gay man. I will feel homophobia—like, I actually physically feel it happening. My stomach will turn into a knot. I start to self-censor and cover. My behaviors and language change immediately. It feels horrible."

Tim and his husband are raising three adorable daughters, and he shared with me how he decides when to share details about the surrogacy process he and his husband undertook to have their girls. Making their own assumptions, many people ask him, "How did the adoption process go for you?" In that moment, Tim has a choice as to whether to correct the person, and he uses a green–yellow–red light self-assessment to make the decision on what to share. He tunes in to see how he's feeling and, based on whether he's feeling green (yes, share) or yellow (pause to think about whether to share) or red (no, don't share), he'll disclose openly, tentatively, or not at all.

I love this approach of using the green–yellow–red light self-assessment when examining the Seven Behavioral Dimensions in moments when we're deciding what and how much to share about ourselves. Checking in with ourselves on an ongoing basis is an essential practice for understanding where we're currently positioned along the Three Selves continuum.

I have the Seven Behavioral Dimensions constantly in mind when I'm determining how authentic I'm being across the Three Selves continuum. For example, when I have a meeting where I'll be pitching business to a new client who is conservative, I actually reflect on my choices across the behavioral dimensions and how this impacts where I'm showing up as my Three Selves. I may be very animated in how I express myself—for example, laughing loudly and using many facial expressions—but then, during the meeting I may find myself being selective in what information I opt to share. For example, when asked the typical "How was your weekend?" small-talk ice-breaker, I may choose to talk about trying a new restaurant and not mention that I was hungover all weekend because I consumed too much wine while out for dinner. I may also speak far more formally by avoiding f-bombs and by dropping the pitch of my voice. In making these choices, some of my behaviors are authentic, and in other ways I'm choosing to behave in a more socially appropriate way for that particular context (which still feels fine because I'm exercising choice to adapt my behavior). But the point here is that I feel alignment in being authentic in some of the dimensions while being adaptive in others—because I'm *choosing* to engage in these behaviors. In living more authentically, the overall objective is to have as many experiences of alignment as possible, which you do through the many individual *choices* you make every day.

I can't emphasize enough that how you choose to live out the Seven Behavioral Dimensions is entirely in your control. You aren't born into one of the Three Selves and required to stay there for life—*you* decide which of these Selves to be, and when, based on how you behave. It's up to you to choose where you are on the continuum in the behavioral dimensions at any given moment. You need to decide to be authentic, to be intentional about behaving in a way that's consistent with your thoughts, your values, your desires, and your inner self. This is very powerful, and we'll spend significant time in the following chapters exploring how you can exercise choice in order to live, work, and lead more joyfully.

2

Your Authentic Self:
Who You'd Be If There Were
No Consequences

it was when I stopped searching for home within others
and lifted the foundations of home within myself
i found there were no roots more intimate
than those between a mind and body
that have decided to be whole.

RUPI KAUR

PAUSE TO reflect on the following: If there were no negative consequences for your behavior...

Who would you be?

How would you behave?

What would you reveal about yourself?

What would you say?

How would you dress?

Who would you love?

Who would you befriend?

What would you do for a living?

What boundaries would you draw?

Your answers to these questions reveal your Authentic Self—the person you would be (the good, the bad, and the ugly) if you didn't live in fear of the negative consequences of being authentic. It's the self that reflects the fusion of your values, beliefs, needs, desires, thoughts, emotions, and traits. You *choose* to express this unique combination—the essence of *you*—by how you show up along the Seven Behavioral Dimensions. The more your actions, how you communicate and emote verbally and non-verbally, your appearance, what you share, and how you interact with others reflect who you are at your core, the more you'll have alignment in how you're thinking, feeling, and behaving. Your Authentic Self is your most elevated and empowered self along the Three Selves continuum.

Your Authentic Self

Description	Key Attributes	How It Feels
Who you would be if there were no negative consequences for your actions	• A reflection of your core values, beliefs, needs, desires, thoughts, emotions, and traits	• Empowering
		• Like alignment
		• Fulfilling
	• You have alignment in how you're thinking, feeling, and behaving	• Liberating
	• You feel belonging in your interactions with others	

Some of you reading this book will already be very self-aware and well acquainted with your Authentic Self, and this is how you show up as much as possible. You are very fortunate, as this is a gift. When you're able to be your Authentic Self, it feels amazing.

For others reading this book, you may not know who your Authentic Self is or you may have lost touch with your Authentic Self. This is a difficult feeling, and you need to do some hard work to discover, or rediscover, who that person is.

Or for others it might be a mix: you have a sense of your Authentic Self in some areas, you're not so sure in other areas, and you often bury your true self and instead show up as the person you think others want you to be.

Whichever group you fall into, in order to live more often as your Authentic Self, it is critical that you engage in self-reflection practices so that you better understand who you are at your core. This means engaging in assertive self-inquiry and asking yourself challenging questions like the ones posed at the beginning of this chapter. Given that what is important to you, your needs and desires, and who you are may change over time, deep and continuous self-reflection will be essential to understanding your true self throughout your life.

In guiding you to uncover key insights about your Authentic Self, let's first help you understand how living authentically *feels* for you.

Authenticity Feels Like Alignment

Authenticity is more than just a thought or a thinking experience—it's a profoundly emotional experience that elicits concrete, physical reactions. Yes, we have thoughts about who we are; what our values, beliefs, needs, and desires are; how we want to behave; and what we want to hold back when sharing. But being immersed in your thoughts can actually get in the way of being authentic. When you're focusing on the thoughts that are swirling in your head (I call these thoughts "The Voice"), you lose awareness of the present moment, which means that you're less inclined to focus on experiencing your surroundings through your senses (e.g., taking in the sights, sounds, and smells in the room, and the feeling of sitting in the chair). You're less aware of the emotional and physical sensations in your body, and because you're not tuning in to how you're feeling, you're missing out on the opportunity to use feelings as a guidepost for practicing authenticity.

In our interview, Dr. Rick Hanson, a neuropsychologist and co-author of the acclaimed book *Buddha's Brain: The Practical Neuroscience of Happiness, Love and Wisdom*, told me, "Authenticity is about congruence and alignment in how you actually feel, how you think you feel, and what you enable others to see. It involves undefendedness, self-disclosure, and vulnerability... When you're not being authentic, it's like living in the gatekeeper's cottage; you don't inhabit the whole of who you are. When you're authentic, you occupy yourself in a total way."

As you've no doubt noticed, when you're tuning in to how you're feeling, you'll experience actual physical sensations in your body—for example, butterflies in the stomach when feeling fear or shame (the yogis know this as third chakra stimulation); heaviness in the chest when feeling anger, contempt, or shame; tingling at the back of the neck when feeling fear; pulsing along the spine when feeling surprise; warm flutters through the heart and chest area when feeling happiness; and a joyous buzz throughout the body when feeling pride. When you're being authentic, you'll feel some of these physical sensations in your body. The inverse is also true: when you're not being true to yourself, you'll feel other physical sensations. That's because authenticity is a physical experience, connected to your emotions as well as your thoughts.

Your awareness of how you're *feeling* is critical for practicing authenticity. In fact, your body will tell you what experience you're having before your mind has even caught up. So, when you're learning to be more of your Authentic Self, it helps to *tune out* your mind and instead *tune in* to your body in order to

- get in touch with the physical side of the experience,
- understand how you're feeling in the moment of being authentic, and

• name the feelings that connect with your Authentic Self.

Many have told me that being authentic feels like an experience of alignment—in how they're thinking, feeling, and behaving. Jai-Jagdeesh, a globally celebrated musician and yogi, told me, "Authenticity feels like spontaneous combustion. When I am doing something that feels resonant in my bones, there are all these feelings of joy and moments of synchronicity in the universe. I feel so alive that I could explode. My whole body system feels it. I don't have to work to breathe deeply, I feel less tension in my body, I feel relaxed." Pam Palmater, a Mi'kmaw professor and activist, told me that she feels the most authentic when she is with her community: "I go to reserves to spend time with my Mi'kmaw elders to do things like feasting, ceremonies, and drumming, because my heartbeat is with my people and it's when I feel most authentic. My heart connects with the drumming—it's a physical and emotional thing—and I feel like crying and sometimes do."

When I'm being my Authentic Self and feel the alignment, it's like I'm actually flying—and that's because, in a way, I am. In an authentic moment my body feels free to express itself in the way it's currently experiencing the moment, and my emotions are true to my body's expression. I often have this feeling of alignment when I'm on stage speaking to an audience that I've really connected with. On stage, I'm almost entirely present and can surrender into the experience. I feel, and am, as authentic as I can be given the environment. Regardless of who is in the room, I feel free to share stories about vulnerable experiences; to use my "potty mouth" (the f-bomb is one of my favorite words); and to fully express my emotions through my eyes, face, and arm gestures (my sister, Komal, says it's like I'm conducting traffic when I speak—fabulous). I feel alive to my core and that's because my words, actions, thoughts, and physical expressions are all in perfect alignment.

Not surprisingly, not only do I feel kick-ass about being true to myself, but others are more engaged with me in those moments than at any other time—in fact, these are the presentations on which I receive the most positive feedback. And of course, now that I know how amazing authentic moments are, I'm committed to having them as often as possible.

Authentic Voices
What Does It Feel Like to Mask Your Authentic Self?

When we're unable to consistently be authentic and instead we're consistently performing, it adversely impacts our mental, physical, and spiritual health. Over the years, I've heard many stories about how conforming and masking has led to adverse health effects—loneliness, anxiety, depression, digestive issues, heartache, headaches, back and chest pain, body tension, and sleep issues are just a few of the examples.

Here's what a few people I interviewed for the book had to say about how masking their Authentic Self feels in their bodies:

"When I notice that I'm holding back, I will pause to ask myself, 'How are you feeling right now?' I'll notice that my breath is shorter, my shoulders are tensing up, and I feel some shade of anxiety. My body knows something's off before my mind catches up, and it's good because then I can use those cues to recalibrate."
Annahid Dashtgard, a leadership and inclusion professional

"When I'm not being true to myself, I instantly feel 'out of body'—I float up to watch it happen."
Heidi Levine, a leader at a global law firm

"When I feel like I'm going off my values, I immediately start to feel uncomfortable. I catch myself feeling bad and then start to ask

myself questions like 'Why do I feel this way?' I'll notice that I have a feeling in my chest. I'm not nauseous, but I feel sick—it's like a feeling of welling up, anxiety, sweatiness, feeling flushed. So I'll then ask myself, 'Does it feel right to you to act like this?'"
Dr. Catherine Zahn, the president and CEO of a world-renowned hospital

Being Authentic Is a Privilege

Not everyone has the opportunity or ability to be their Authentic Self as often as they would like along all the Seven Behavioral Dimensions. Yes, technically everyone has a choice, but some have circumstances that make exercising the choice to be authentic more difficult—from financial constraints to family and religious expectations to concerns about safety. For example, a mother who wants to pursue her passions in life but can't until her children are older; a Jewish adult who wishes to convert to another faith but fears being ostracized from his family; a man who wants to wear makeup and gender non-conforming clothing but fears for his safety; a person in financial need who wants to quit his job but can't; a new junior employee in an organization who wants to speak out more often and disagree with team members but feels she'll be reprimanded if she does; or the only woman on a team who doesn't want to learn how to play golf but feels that she has to in order to get invited to company events. Having the ability to choose to be your Authentic Self more consistently than others affords you privilege.

I had the opportunity to interview Nina,* a hardworking professional who is passionate about her role and career path. She

* Not her real name

lives with chronic pain syndrome, which includes conditions related to women's health issues. In our moving discussion, Nina described how her disability impacts her physical health and how, at certain points in her life, managing high pain levels affected her ability to be employed and her ability to live authentically. She told me: "I knew who I was and I knew that I had so much to offer, but I had great difficulty tapping into this. I felt isolated because I couldn't fulfill my dreams. If I was healthy, I would be better able to bring my authenticity to bear on all my interactions. How can you truly be yourself when you can't get out of bed on most days? How can you truly be yourself when you can't make a living?"

Our discussion opened my eyes to the lived experiences of people who genuinely want to scream from treetops about their Authentic Self, but on many days physically cannot. Authenticity is a privilege for those of us who can scream whenever we want.

Many have told me that as they have become more senior, both in age and profession, it gets easier to be themselves at home, work, and play. Why? Because they are older, have financial stability, have job security, have more personal and professional autonomy, have more access to societal power, and, quite frankly, they don't give a hoot anymore about being judged because years of masking made them feel crappy and taught them to care less about how others see them. In other words, those with higher status, power, and success are often better positioned to practice authenticity more consistently than others.

Before I move on, just one more quick word on age—if it's getting easier for you to be authentic as a "boomer," it's probably a combination of all the aforementioned factors and your brain at work. Research has shown that if you keep your brain healthy, it tends to organize and process differently as it gets to middle age, which includes making better, more complex decisions effectively.[1]

Getting Comfortable with the Uncomfortable

In your exploration to discover (or rediscover) your Authentic Self, you will undoubtedly find that parts of this journey are uncomfortable for you. Some of your discomfort may come from knowing that others will have negative judgments about your wants and desires. You may fear that being your Authentic Self will cause people to feel that you should change the way you emote or speak, or to wish you wouldn't share your opinions so openly.

Some of your discomfort may come from the fact that aspects of your Authentic Self, and the ways in which you would show up across the behavioral dimensions if there were no consequences, are, frankly, unpleasant. It just is what it is. As your mama told you, no one is perfect (not even us perfectionists), and so there are undoubtedly things about you that are off-putting, annoying, and disagreeable. For example, if you have a very bad temper, you're arrogant, you love sexist jokes, or sometimes you're really mean to others, this can be hard to face up to and own. What to do about the unpleasant aspects of who we are can be tricky and challenging, and we'll discuss this more when we look closely at the Adapted Self; but for now, just be ready to meet and acknowledge some of the less-pleasant parts of yourself. As it has been said, "No man is worse for knowing the worst of himself."[2]

Some aspects of your Authentic Self may be uncomfortable for you because you were told that they are bad and ugly sides of you. Somewhere along the way you may have internalized messaging that your values or desires or preferred ways of behaving are the "wrong way to be." As a result of this conditioning, you feel flawed because you possess these traits and so you constantly seek to push these traits down.

As you'll recall from the Introduction, growing up I was repeatedly told that my gregarious energy and expressiveness were "bad ways" of behaving. I came to think that they are "bad" sides of my Authentic Self. So I learned from a young age to change my behavior in order to conform to what others expected of me (across the behavioral dimensions, I learned to significantly alter how I expressed my emotions, how I communicated non-verbally, and how I spoke). Because of this, for years I struggled with how much of my energy and expressiveness I should share with others. I worried that if I shared too much, others wouldn't like to be around me. I used to envision a ball of light, which represented my energy, with a rope tied around it. In situations where I'd be meeting someone new who seemed a bit closed off, I'd actually imagine myself pulling the rope in toward myself in order to "rein in" my energy so that the person would be more likely to like me.

In my journey with authenticity, I've now learned to release the rope entirely, because I realized the issue isn't my energy (in fact, living like the Energizer Bunny is pretty fabulous). The issue is the messaging, which I had internalized, that a high level of energy and expressiveness is bad. I've learned to let go of the negative messaging that these are "bad" sides of my Authentic Self and to replace it with self-embracing thinking: that these attributes are wonderful aspects of my Authentic Self.

In your own exploration of your Authentic Self, it is so important to accept the uncomfortable, unpleasant, and disagreeable "stuff" that you uncover about yourself. Your initial impulse may be to rail against what you uncover, and that's normal. But ultimately embracing all aspects of who you are—even the unpleasant aspects—is a fundamental step on your path to living more authentically. The reality is that when we deny, fight, or minimize attributes about ourselves that are hard for us to face or admit to, they don't disappear or go away. And if we don't address them in a healthy way, they often turn into self-limiting beliefs and behaviors. When we become fixated on masking aspects of ourselves that we don't like or think that others may not like, we move away from shining in the areas that do make us feel good about ourselves. In essence, the effort you expend to mask your Authentic Self doesn't contribute to making you a better person.

Despite the Adverse Side Effects, Do It Anyway

When you begin to discover and increasingly show up as who you really are along the Seven Behavioral Dimensions, others may not like it. They're used to the "you" who conforms and masks to get along and fit in. Understandably then, it can be a big adjustment for others, and even a shock, to interact with the authentic you. So choosing to be authentic may have negative consequences that you didn't want or expect to incur, such as rejection, judgment, conditional love, and career stagnation.

Some of the people I interviewed told me that living more authentically meant that others didn't want to interact with them any longer, that doors to certain opportunities closed, and that they lost membership in a social tribe. Kelvin Tran, the senior vice president and chief auditor for a global bank, told me that when he started to practice being more authentic, others seemed uncomfortable with this change. When I asked him why, he replied, "People who aren't ready to bring their whole selves to work feel uncomfortable around your honesty. They think, 'I would never share that,' and they don't connect with you because of it. But someone who is authentic loves your truthfulness. It's contagious."

In my journey with living more authentically, I've found that others haven't always been crazy about the emergence of "Authentic Ritu." Several years ago, I took a three-month sabbatical from my fancy law firm job to complete a yoga teacher training at an ashram in India, which taught me a formal structure and practice for self-reflection. Wow, did my life ever change after this experience. After spending hours and hours meditating on and contemplating who I truly am and how better to embrace this, I felt different, and I had a clear understanding of how I wanted to behave differently across the dimensions, in a way that was truer to my core. But I came home to the same relationships and the same job in the same hardcore corporate world. The people I had left at home were not expecting the "new Ritu" (in fact, one of my friends even coined my new way of being as "PAR," which stood for Post-Ashram Ritu).

If it was hard for me to practice being more authentic in my existing relationships and job, it was even harder for some of the people in my life who didn't expect my changed way of being. It meant that boundaries in relationships changed. I transitioned out of old relationships (a nice way of saying "broke up with people"—and I've never looked back) while transitioning into new ones, and I left the world of being a corporate employee, where my spirit was being quashed, to launch my own business. I relished the benefits of being more *me*, but the undesired side effects were hard at times—for example, some people didn't like PAR and told me so or, to put it bluntly, didn't want to be my friend anymore.

Ultimately, because of the personal costs that come with embracing your authenticity, you may feel compelled to show up as your Performing Self. As global inclusion speaker and author Verna Myers told me, "If we choose to show up as our true selves, we run the risk of making others feel insecure or uncomfortable because it may not accord with their views or they're forced to step out of their presumption of who we should be. We make their world harder. And because we know this happens, we may choose to be someone else or to mask. And sometimes we don't even notice that we're modifying our behavior to minimize the cost of being authentic."

Like any journey, practicing authenticity may at times feel like an uphill ride fraught with costs, pitfalls, and obstacles. As with any journey, keeping the goal in mind motivates us to keep going even when it feels very challenging. People who choose to live by the Authenticity Principle continually weigh the upside and downside of being true to themselves, and in the end they consistently choose to be themselves, even when it means changing relationships, jobs, and life circumstances. These people are able to do this largely because they have a very good sense of who their Authentic Self is, which they've developed through engaging in a range of self-reflection practices. We'll now explore how you can make this happen in the next chapter, which focuses on self-reflection strategies and self-inquiry questions.

3

Get to Know
Your Authentic Self

You must learn to be a diver if you wish to discover pearls.
RUMI

PAULEANNA REID, a millennial who is a motivational speaker and author, was invited to present on a panel along with more-senior women leaders about empowerment. While waiting in the greenroom in the presence of very educated, accomplished women, Pauleanna noticed that she was the youngest in the group. Feelings of inadequacy washed over her as she contemplated what she could speak about that would impress them. Fear and vulnerability almost immobilized her. But once onstage, she made the choice to "be real." She said to herself, "F*ck it, I'm going to choose to do me," and she decided to speak from the heart, persisting through her insecurities. The more Pauleanna was herself, the better she felt; and the better she felt, the more comfortable she felt about being herself. She was a dynamo onstage, which I know because I was in the audience and this is how I met her.

In our deeply moving conversation, Pauleanna told me, "Authenticity is about living life without a mask on, without needing to look over my shoulder when I'm being me." As a public speaker, Pauleanna bravely shares her experiences with anxiety, depression, and sexual violence. "I openly tell my story to audiences—I don't hide—as part of living my truth every day." And in fact, Pauleanna's experiences have contributed to her passion for living more authentically.

Pauleanna's journey of learning to be more of herself hasn't been an easy one. She described to me how, growing up, she felt intense pressure to conform to her parents' expectations, while in her mind she felt "wild." She explained that she often felt confused about the mixed messaging she received: "When I was young, my parents often told me, 'You be who you want and [you] can do anything you want to.' But then as I grew up, the rules changed and I heard, 'You can't do this or that or be this or that . . . My parents pressured me to conform. Especially as a woman in my culture, I was conditioned to be strong, but that also meant shutting my mouth and hiding my truth. And I was worried about disgracing my parents and family members."

Pauleanna also faced many painful moments growing up, which impacted her ability to live more authentically. As a Black girl, she experienced racist bullying that made her feel like an outsider among her peers (which was layered on top of her feelings of disconnection from her family). She shared with me that she consistently felt feelings of worthlessness: "I cried myself to sleep most nights and woke up daily hoping to die." She was unsure about who she ought to be. "I befriended the wrong crowds because it was 'safer' than being their enemy," she told me. Deeply needing to feel loved and desired, Pauleanna found herself in a number of harrowing situations. At the age of fourteen, she went to a dance with a boy she had been introduced to and was raped by him at the end of the evening. At the age of eighteen, she had an abortion due to an unwanted pregnancy and found herself in a physically abusive relationship with an MVP of a sports team.

The turning point for Pauleanna came after her second suicide attempt while she was in college. In her "desire to die but not feel any pain doing it," Pauleanna lifted her foot to jump in front of a moving subway car, but a man who was standing behind her grabbed the loop of her backpack and dragged her to the ground. "I thank God that he stopped me," she says now. "He is an angel." After that experience, Pauleanna realized she felt lost in her life and that she wanted to find her way back to herself. This led her to commit to figuring out who her Authentic Self is and to living a life of being true to herself, her needs and desires, and all of what is important to her.

In sharing her story with me, Pauleanna noted that without the negative experiences she went through, she would not be the woman she is proud to be today. While they have fueled her anxiety and depression, they also have contributed to her passion for living more authentically. In particular, she noted that "People know so much about others, but they don't know enough about themselves. The first step to living authentically is to get to know yourself. You do this by spending time alone, by learning about yourself, by romancing yourself by going for dinner with yourself—get to know who you really are."

Pauleanna's thoughtful insights highlight a key aspect of the Authenticity Principle: in order to be more of who you truly are, you *must* come to know yourself. You must do the introspective work that's necessary to better understand who you are and then be yourself, first and foremost, *with* yourself. You will have an exceptionally hard—and, dare I say, impossible—time being authentic with others if you're not authentic with yourself first.

Use Self-Reflection Practices to Know Yourself

In my conversation with Dr. Rick Hanson, the neuropsychologist and author of *Buddha's Brain* I mentioned in chapter 2, he emphasized that authentic people are more self-aware and committed to self-regulation. Authentic people are aware of the whole of who they are—which includes having a very good understanding of how they feel and tolerating these feelings, especially the dark ones.

Well, isn't this just it? If you don't know who you are—and more specifically, what your values, needs, desires, traits, thoughts, and emotions are (I call these the "Who I am markers")—how will you know how you ought to behave in order to reflect your Authentic Self and Adapted Self?

When you know who your Authentic Self is, you're more likely to anchor to your "Who I am markers" and use them as beacons for how to behave. Even in situations where you strategically choose to alter your behavior, you have these markers in your mind. For example, if being kind is a value you hold dearly, then when someone makes a joke in front of you about overweight people, your "Who I am markers" will signal to your mind and body: "This doesn't feel right! Say or do something." You'll feel the tension in your body and your mind will be flooded with possible things to say. Even though you may feel discomfort with calling out the person who made the joke, you'll do it anyway because of your "Who I am markers"—they pulse within you. You may alter how you do it—for example, you may start by asking a question like "Sorry, what did you mean by that?" rather than saying, "WTF was that?!" which is actually what you want to say. But you will be authentic; you won't perform by remaining silent or laughing at the joke.

The clear path to better understanding your Authentic Self is to engage in self-reflection practices. And by self-reflection practices, I'm referring to formal activities and experiences that raise the level of awareness you have about yourself. What follows is a comprehensive list of self-reflection activities and experiences (including a few specific examples of what each can look like) that will provide you with formal opportunities to better understand your Authentic Self.

- **Meditation:** seated, walking, silent
- **Mindfulness experiences:** activities in nature, yoga retreats
- **Exercise:** yoga, walking, running, team sports
- **Adventurous moments:** outside-the-box travel and experiences like skydiving
- **Creative pursuits:** drawing, painting, dancing, drumming
- **Writing:** journaling, writing poetry and stories
- **Therapy:** individual, group
- **Coaching:** working with a life or leadership coach
- **Self-guided learning:** reading, courses, research
- **Group-guided experiences:** talk-circles, men's groups, sweat lodges
- **Seeking feedback:** constructive input and advice from family, friends, and colleagues
- **Teaching others:** parenting, mentoring, lecturing

Authentic Voices
What Do People Do to Get to Know Themselves?

Here's what some of the people I interviewed for this book said they do to better understand their "Who I am markers":

"People don't know this about me, but I practice yoga every day. At first I didn't tell people because it would have been outside the mainstream. Now I do—I don't care if someone thinks it's weird

because yoga has been liberating. I close my eyes and go within."
Rob Granatstein, managing partner of a global law firm

"Here are some of the exercises I ask my clients to do when they desire better perspective about themselves and/or their work: spend time in an open space (e.g., the ocean or mountainside) to take in things larger than themselves; spend time writing regularly; turn off technology during the day for forty-five to seventy minutes in order to go deeper on a topic; use different practices of meditation; spend time alone, even if it's on a plane. These spaces of self-reflection have personally helped me to dive into places that require vulnerability."
Charles Lee, the CEO of an ideas execution firm and author

"The first step for self-exploration is to take care of your physical self. I was in India a few months ago and I decided to take care of my physical self. I started going to the gym, seeing a dietician, eating well. I needed to do this to get myself to a better place for self-exploration. And of course, all of this is worth it because I am worth it."
Deepa Mehta, an award-winning director and screenwriter

"I put myself into reflective and challenging situations. I attend retreats with people who share my identity as a Black man and I've participated in a Native American sweat lodge . . . It's also helped to have conversations with others. I've talked to lots of people—mentors, work colleagues, my wife. I've done lots of reading of self-help books, and in particular about breaking the chains of slavery and White supremacy."
Dr. Eddie Moore Jr., an activist and educator

The mere thought of these types of activities might make you feel itchy.

Maybe you've heard about them mostly from "mushy" self-help gurus, hippies, yogis, and tree huggers, and because of this, it's hard for you to take such activities seriously. But here we are now, equipped with extensive research and data that say these "crunchy" self-reflection practices are invaluable in helping to increase our happiness.

Maybe you're uncomfortable about doing the tough work that could expose some of your inner demons in the process of discovering aspects of your Authentic Self. It might mean changing the way you live, who you love, where you work, who you play with, and so on. Discovering your Authentic Self means opening up to yourself, which for many can be a scary, vulnerable feeling, and so you might think it's easier and safer to avoid it altogether.

Maybe you're so used to living in a distracted state that self-reflection activities are foreign to you. You're not used to putting down your smartphone, turning off your computer and TV, holding off on posting your curated stuff on social media, pausing from reading others' curated stuff, not drinking another bottle of wine, or being by yourself. These activities will require that you reduce the noise you create in your life, and the intoxicants you take in to numb yourself, so that you can hear the thoughts in your head and feel the sensations in your body.

Or maybe you do think self-reflection is valuable, but you haven't been taught how to do it effectively. If so, you're not alone on this. I frequently ask my global audiences, "Given how important self-reflection is to personal and professional development, how many of you ever had someone sit you down—at school or home or anywhere else—to say, this is why self-reflection is important and this is how to do it?" In an audience of a few hundred, maybe ten hands will go up.

A key point here is that most of us need help to access our thoughts and feelings, to feel more creative and centered, and to get to the core of knowing who we are. We need formal self-reflection practices to manage the madness. Think about the non-stop noise inside you and around you: The Voice chattering in your head, people yelling, street noise, office noise, dinging social media/e-mail/text messages. And you may not stop the busy-ness of your life unless there's something that's forcing you to—like going to a therapy session or a painting class you've paid for. You need regular, practical ways to quiet your mind, providing you with room to shift gears and give thought to who you truly are.

These kinds of practices actually have a science to them. They trigger areas of the brain that push us away from the madness and into being centered. Yes, adopting formal self-reflection practices adds another "must do" to your already crowded list of tasks, but they are essential for better knowing who you are (and they have many other mental, physical, and spiritual benefits as well).

I particularly value the self-reflection experiences of therapy, yoga and spiritual retreats, meditation, reflective journaling, hiking, and dancing. I engage in some of these activities while I'm listening to my favorite music or I'm somewhere in nature, and sometimes even when I'm stressed beyond words and at my desk, on a plane, or sitting in traffic. These practices help me to breathe deeper, feel more relaxed, hear the thoughts in my head more clearly, and be honest about what I truly feel and think about who I am.

My hope is that if you have an aversion to, or simply just haven't been engaging in, self-reflection, this will change for you after reading this book. And, like with many of the other strategies I'll discuss in the book, I recommend starting small and then going big. Self-reflection doesn't have to start with one big question— "Who am I?" or "What do I really want?"—but can begin with one or two smaller questions that get you thinking and feeling more deeply.

Let's begin with having you reflect on how you'll make more space for self-reflection in your life going forward.

Reflection Moment

- Which of the self-reflection activities and experiences listed above will you engage in to help you better know yourself?

- To ensure that you embed these practices into your life:
  - When will you engage in these practices?
  - Where will you engage in these practices?
  - How will you hold yourself accountable for engaging in these practices?

Why Is Authentic Living Important for You?

It's imperative to know *why* you want to live more authentically. When you're aware of your drivers for change, you're more likely to alter your behavior, especially when the drivers are intrinsic (internally motivated) versus extrinsic (externally motivated). With this powerful knowledge, you'll have clarity about why living authentically is important to you and you'll want to anchor to it and connect it to the outcomes you desire, all of which will increase the likelihood of you acting on what's motivating you.

For some, there will be a catalyst or event that inspires you to want to live differently. For example, Sean Tompkins, the CEO of a UK-headquartered global real estate and construction organization, shared with me that he decided to change the way he was living after his wife nearly died and then was in a coma for six weeks after giving birth to their second child. For others, there may not be a singular, pivotal moment that will push them toward authenticity, but over time they'll come to a place where they see that they need to choose to live differently. It won't necessarily be one thing that particularly stands out—it could be a combination of factors that causes them to realize they're lacking personal, relational, and/or professional joy.

Pause to explore why living authentically is important for you.

Reflection Moment

- What are the three things you most love about your life?
- What three things would you change about your life, if you could?
- What do you stand to gain from living more authentically? Conversely, what do you stand to lose if you don't live your life in a more authentic way?

Exploring the "Who I Am Markers"

Have you ever stopped to ask yourself, "Who am I?" It's a daunting, monumental question. As mentioned just above, starting off by exploring more focused, specific questions can be a more effective way to begin, especially if engaging in self-reflection isn't part of your regular practice. And more focused, specific questions can get you to the same result of asking the big "Who am I?" question.

Take a moment to reflect on your "Who I am markers."

Reflection Moment

- What five words would you use to describe yourself?

- Complete these statements:
  - I shine the most when...
  - I feel the most connected to myself when...

- What are the three things that you most wish others knew about you?

- What three things would you change about yourself if you could?

- If you could wave a magic wand and do absolutely anything in this world without restriction in your...
  - Personal life: What would you do? How would you be living? Why?
  - Relationships: What would you do? Who would you let go? Who would you connect with? Why?
  - Professional life: What would you do? How would you earn a living? Why?

What Is Important to You?

Your values are the compass that guides how you behave in your life. They are at the root of who you are and, therefore, it's critical that you identify what your values are and how your behaviors reflect your values. As Verna Myers, a global inclusion speaker and author, said, "To be authentic, you have to know what your values are. Your values steer your decisions; they show you what matters to you, the way you want people to be with you, what gets you upset, how you want people to treat you, what you learned growing up, what appeals to you, what makes you happy, how you make judgments, who you respect."

Authentic Voices
Identifying Your Values

To help you identify your values, here are two approaches that were shared with me in the interviews I did for this book:

"**First, write** down thirty 'life insights' you've learned through experience (e.g., Feel free to dismiss the judgments of anyone who is

not as happy as you are). Second, for each of your insights, identify the 'foundational values' represented by that insight and write
them down. For example, for the insight given above, you could
identify the values of self-respect, critical thinking, and resilience.
Third, after doing that for each insight, you should end up with a
list of thirty to ninety foundational values. You will notice some are
repeated over and over again. Clearly, those values are the ones
most important to you."
Drew Dudley, a global leadership speaker

"I keep track through journaling of things that come up over the
course of a day: What did I love? What did I loathe? It paints a clear
picture of what drives and motivates me, as well as what perhaps
drains my energy. I then use these insights to reflect on how they align
with my values and who I am at my core. For example, I love coaching
because it reflects my value of enabling others to see their potential, value, and worth. I dislike gossip because it violates this value."
Michelle Grocholsky, a talent management leader and coach

Now that you've seen how others tune in to their personal
values to build their awareness of who they are, reflect on the
qualities that are most important to you.

Reflection Moment
- What are your five key needs and desires? Ask yourself: what
  does my heart want?
- What are your five top values?
- How are these values reflected in your behavior?

Exploring the Behaviors of Your Authentic Self

People who can clearly identify how they're currently behaving, why they behave the way they do, and how they actually want to behave are better able to successfully alter their future behavior. (It's also a core aspect of emotional intelligence, the ability to identify your own and others' emotions and to better manage and adjust your emotions based on the environment, other people, and your own needs.)

In our discussion, Sonya Kunkel, the chief inclusion officer and vice president of people strategies at a global bank, told me that taking deliberate steps to change your behavior is key to living more authentically. She described the following practice that she uses: you divest yourself of things in your life that no longer serve you, that are not aligned with your values, or that don't assist you in living and leading authentically. For example, the last time Sonya engaged in this process in her life was several years ago—she sold her house, adjusted some relationships, and eventually changed jobs. She knew she needed to make changes because she wasn't living authentically. As she explained to me, "This process opened up room to be myself and, since then, I bought a farm (which was a childhood dream), I found the love of my life, and I've been creating cultural change within my industry."

Now let's take a moment to have you reflect on your behaviors, and more specifically, the authentic behaviors you wish you could engage in.

Reflection Moment
Complete the following statements:

- If I felt truly free to be my Authentic Self, my life would look like...

- If I felt truly free to be my Authentic Self, I would...
  - immediately start to...
  - scream from the treetops that...
  - accept that...
  - finally tell...
  - immediately stop...
  - stop holding back...
  - stop telling myself to...
  - release...

IN ADDITION to the many other insightful comments Paule-anna Reid shared with me during our conversation, she said: "We have the choice to live a mediocre life or an abundant life, which goes back to if you're living your truth." In order to figure out what your truth is, you must lift yourself out of the thick fog that's hampering your line of sight to your Authentic Self. You must do the work to better understand who your Authentic Self is and why living authentically is important to you. This is precisely what the self-reflection strategies and questions in this chapter have been designed to help you with.

To better enable you to live more authentically, in the next several chapters we'll delve into what is holding you back from doing so by exploring the Performing Self and what is leading you to conform and mask who you are. We'll come back to the Adapted Self (and, of great significance, how to flow between your Authentic Self and Adapted Self and leverage the Seven Behavioral Dimensions) later in the book.

4

Your Performing Self: You Lack Choice, So You Conform and Mask

My friend, I am not what I seem. Seeming is but a
garment I wear—a care-woven garment that protects me from
thy questionings and thee from my negligence.

KHALIL GIBRAN

A LARGE ORGANIZATION hired me a few years ago to help its senior leaders become more inclusive. I really enjoyed my work with this team, except for my experience with one of the executives, who is an older White man. He was reputed to be difficult, which was borne out in our work together. He had a surface-level interest in becoming more inclusive, and this was very clear from our interactions.

Last year, I had meetings at the client's office and ran into this leader in the reception area upon my arrival. In his booming voice, he said, "Hello, Ritu. How are you doing?" That's all it took—I instantly felt my neck and shoulder muscles tighten. As part of our polite small talk, which lasted for a few minutes, he asked me what I'd been up to. Thinking that this would be a safe, easy topic, I told him that I had just returned from a vacation to a Caribbean island. Unbeknownst to me, the island is one of his favorite vacation destinations, and so he began to pepper me with questions about where I stayed, ate, visited, shopped, and so on.

For me, this holiday was unique because I had gone to the island with my friends who are originally from there. I didn't experience the island as an affluent tourist, as he clearly had; I had enjoyed it through the eyes of people who live there. I did some touristy stuff, but mostly I ate home-cooked meals, hung out with uncles and aunties, and sat on back porches. It was lovely, but clearly very different than what this leader expected I had done.

So, with a forced smile and my Performing Self "friendly voice" (which is probably one octave higher than I normally would speak), I kept repeating, "No, I didn't go there" and "No, I didn't do that." The more I did this, the more he probed to figure out just what in the hell I actually had done while on vacation. I could feel my cheeks getting hotter and my body getting tenser. As we chatted and I kept saying "No," my mind was saying, "Tell him that you went with friends and you did xyz." But I couldn't bring myself to do it. I couldn't tell him that I had a lovely time because I feared it wouldn't be lovely in his eyes. I feared his judgment—that because I didn't stay, eat, or play in any of the fancy places he was mentioning, I was "less than" (and I already had this feeling thanks to his dismissive attitude during our earlier work experience). I felt unsafe to be me with this person.

So instead I performed. My "no's" turned into questions about all the places he had been to. I asked him where I should stay and eat the next time. By the end of our chat, I was speaking about ten octaves higher, laughing as though he was the funniest man on Earth, and oozing pleasantries about all that he had to say.

Afterward my tummy felt queasy, my skin was hot, and my muscles were tight. I had caught my Performing Self in action; I'd watched it all unfold. Even though I knew in the moment that it would have felt better for me to be my Authentic Self (which would have been me telling him exactly what I did) or even my Adapted Self (which would have been me telling him that I went with friends who are from there and giving him some snippets), I couldn't bring myself to do it. My fear led me to perform in order to protect myself, which didn't serve me because I wasn't able to honor my truth.

And here was another enlightening insight for me: Upon returning from the trip, I told several other people (including clients) *exactly* what I had done while I was away. I was authentic in sharing with them because I felt safe to be myself with them.

Afterwards, I told this story to several of my friends, emphasizing how I had caught myself performing. Interestingly, a few of them said the same thing in response: that if I had been authentic, not only might the executive have thought my time on the island was lovely but, more importantly, he may have left our conversation coveting a similar experience and it would have been a learning moment for him on several fronts. I hadn't even considered this. I was so caught up in my fear of judgment that I hadn't given thought to how being authentic would have set me free and could have been beneficial for both of us.

THE MOST challenging and disheartening of the Three Selves is the Performing Self.

Your Performing Self is the "you" who conforms—both knowingly and unknowingly—by behaving in ways that are outside of how you actually *want* to behave. Being your Performing Self will feel like you're acting, playing a role, or masking who you truly are in order to protect yourself. It's a facade—a construction of a persona or image that you project to others. It consists of behaviors you engage in because you feel like you *have to* and not because you *want to*. *You feel like you don't have a choice but to conform or mask.* And, because you lack choice, it feels disempowering.

Your Performing Self

Description	Key Attributes	How It Feels
Who you show up as when you feel you don't have a choice but to conform or mask who you are	• You feel like you lack choice on how to behave • Fear takes away your ability to be who you truly are • You conform—alter your behavior to "fit in" • You mask—hide aspects of who you are • Cultivates feelings of "fitting in" in your interactions with others, but not belonging	• Disempowering • Like misalignment • Disconnecting • Unfulfilling • Exclusionary • Hurtful • Threatening • Exhausting

This is what makes the Performing Self different than the Adapted Self (two key ways: the role of choice, and how it makes you feel). With the Adapted Self, you willingly exercise choice to change how you behave; it's in the service of your needs and others' needs, and so you feel good about your choices. With the Performing Self, you act in certain ways because you're fearful that if you don't alter your behavior or don't mask who you are, you'll experience personal and/or professional rejection, isolation, and more. The Performing Self is the self where you feel the most disconnected, unfulfilled, and powerless because *fear* removes your choice or ability to be who you truly are. As your Performing Self, you feel misaligned and disempowered.

Some may argue that we always have the choice to be who we truly are. However, the reality is that the ability to exercise *real* choice in being authentic isn't accessible to all of us in every moment. For example, because we fear alienation, financial consequences, threats to our safety, or being disowned. Recall that the ability to be authentic is a privilege.

Sometimes you know you're performing—you deliberately play a role. And other times you don't know you're performing—the fear response and the protection centers of your unconscious brain kick in and you behave in ways that your brain believes will keep you safe from harm. Some people may unknowingly default to the Performing Self if they haven't engaged in extensive self-reflection practices, as discussed in chapter 3, and they don't know who their Authentic Self is. In these cases, people come across as being highly constructed in how they present themselves and it feels obvious to us that they're performing—they seem "phony" or "fake."

What's important to recognize here is that every single one of us at various points in our life's journey will experience situations in which we lack real choice because of our fear of negative consequences (real or perceived) of exercising that choice. And because of this, we primarily do one of two things, if not both:

- We conform, which means we begrudgingly alter how we act along the Seven Behavioral Dimensions in order to meet the behavioral expectations that we feel others have of us.
- We mask, which means we hide aspects of who we are in order to shield against judgment or to meet our perception of others' expectations.

When you perform, you often have inner conflict between how you want to show up and what you're actually doing. This conflict may manifest itself with such thoughts as "I feel like a fake," "Am I selling out?" or "I hate myself for being like this!" Performing will cause you to feel confused, frustrated, disconnected, unfulfilled, and powerless because you lack the ability, or the real choice, to be who you truly are. And because performing doesn't feel good, it takes up energy—it's exhausting. Not surprisingly, this is exactly what the people I interviewed told me, as you'll see in the upcoming pages.

Fitting In vs. Belonging

The push to conform and mask who we are can be difficult to fight because belonging is an extremely powerful and deep-seated driver for all of us. As social beings, we crave the need to not only *be* part of a tribe but to *feel* part of it. The tribe you want to belong to may be your family, cultural community, circle of friends, neighborhood, social networks, classmates, colleagues, professional associations, volunteer organizations, and those with whom you share pastimes. Through belonging, we experience feelings of acceptance, love, connection, meaning, purpose, inclusion, kinship, and more. But belonging actually isn't about fitting in, which some of us mistakenly believe it to be—it's about being accepted for who we are.

In Brené Brown's important book on vulnerability, *The Gifts of Imperfection*, she shares her insights on the significance of belonging, which she defines as "the innate human desire to be part of something larger than us." She notes that "fitting in is about assessing a situation and becoming who you need to be to be accepted. Belonging, on the other hand, doesn't require us to *change* who we are; it requires us to *be* who we are." [1]

As Brown eloquently highlights, we are inclined to alter our behavior to become whoever we need to be in order to fit in and be accepted into a tribe. Our desire to belong may cause us to perform so that we can better access the experiences and feelings that come with membership in a tribe. The challenge is that, when we perform in order to belong, we're not accepted based on who we truly are. It is a false sense of belonging, which causes us to feel continued pressure to conform and mask—because if we don't, our membership in the tribe may be threatened.

And this difference between fitting in and belonging strikes at the heart of the Authenticity Principle: the Performing Self is about fitting in because you feel that you have to change your behavior or mask who you are in order to be accepted by others, while the Authentic Self and the Adapted Self are about belonging because you've chosen to behave in such a way that reflects your authenticity and needs, and others have accepted you on the basis of this truth.

In practicing authenticity and fulfilling your related desire to belong to a range of social tribes, it's essential that you have a clear understanding of

- why you seek membership in a particular tribe,
- to what extent you are able to be your Authentic Self and Adapted Self in order to belong in that tribe, and
- the negative impact of performing.

Key message here: never let fitting in take the place of true belonging.

The Performing Self in Action

Life coach and yoga teacher Brigid Dineen told me that some people who we think are living authentically are in fact "fighting quiet battles we know nothing about," because they put on armor to hide their fears and pain, and curate a life that they project to others. Brigid's words resonated with me, because that was my story before I started to live by the Authenticity Principle.

I became a master at living as my Performing Self—a self I created as a shield to guard myself against my vulnerabilities and what I thought would be negative judgments about who I truly am. My Performing Self was all about appearing in a way that I defined as being flawless—strong, confident, and successful—with a thick veneer of positivity, which meant lots of smiling and an "Everything is amazing" type of response to most questions, so that people would think I was far happier than I actually was. I fixated on dressing impeccably to signal class privilege, attractiveness, and that "I have my shit together." Even in the way I spoke, I often masked to hide my insecurities about my abilities and my cultural background. I also conformed in how I spoke in order to fit in with certain social groups by taking on a more formal tenor, dropping the pitch of my voice, and using fancier words.

I knowingly and unknowingly cultivated a cross-section of interests that enabled me to socialize with people I authentically wanted to be around and whose love helped me to develop personal power (including dear friends with whom I could do things like party at hip-hop clubs and bhangra jams, play mas in Trinidad for Carnival, and attend yoga and mindfulness retreats), while at the same time, enabled me to hobnob with other people with whom I felt disconnected but who gave me access to social power. This meant dating men who I could "check boxes" with, attending fundraising events for causes that didn't resonate with me, going to dinners where I'd drink Barolo and eat sous-vide steak while talking about things from different galaxies even though I was the one who felt like the alien, and sitting in box seats to watch hockey games that I could not have cared less about.

And of course, I was highly selective in what I shared with people. I packaged up areas of my life that felt safe to share and that helped to reinforce my image of flawlessness. In moments, I was even performing "authenticity." I would try to signal "Look how real I am" by sprinkling small aspects of my Authentic Self into my overarching Performing Self disposition. For example, I chose to wear bright colors in the business world to signal "I'm so anti-conformist," and I'd talk openly about my love for hip-hop music. But in the areas that truly mattered for my happiness and reflected who I was—like sharing that I grew up in a household run by immigrant parents (which for us meant practices such as reusing foil, clipping coupons, etc.), or sharing my views on social justice, or sharing how extremely insecure and flawed I felt on most days—I masked. Even when I would share my vulnerabilities, they, too, were packaged in such a way that I would give just enough to signal "See, I'm real" while protecting my real pain from being seen or felt by myself and others.

My Performing Self was in full effect. I felt like I *had to* construct this persona in order to protect myself. I didn't feel like I had a choice. In fact, the more I performed, the less choice I felt I had to be authentic or adaptive.

It is said that "you don't know what you don't know." I didn't know that I was living as my Performing Self much of the time. Once I realized it, the real journey of exploring, understanding, and actually being my Authentic Self began.

ALL OF us construct our lives to some degree by knowingly and unknowingly choosing the curated life, persona, image, or face we want to project. Many of us want to show, or we feel pressure to show, that we're leading positive lives (think "keeping up with the Joneses"); we want to look happy, successful, affluent, smart, beautiful, fit, and connected to others. This means packaging up a mishmash of things about ourselves, each of which is either true, adapted but true, mostly true, somewhat true, we wish it were true, kinda sorta not really true, or so totally not true, and putting it all out there.

We perform in myriad ways along the Seven Behavioral Dimensions: how we dress; how we communicate verbally and non-verbally (including the words we use and how we speak); how we treat people; who we associate with and who we avoid; what we say yes/no/maybe to.

We perform by how we emote, constantly smiling or laughing to feign being happy even though we're not; expressing frustration or anger to hide our sadness; projecting a calm, cool, collected demeanor to shield us from having to reveal our insecurities and vulnerabilities; acting like we're effectively managing the stress and pressure we're feeling while we're actually living with high anxiety or depression.

We perform by how much we reveal about our backgrounds, for example: hiding details about what we do in our spare time that would disclose aspects of our identity for which we fear judgment, like our political leaning; acting like we know all about a fancy hobby even though we've never really done it; using humor or bravado to deflect attention from what we perceive to be "deficiencies" we possess, like being particularly short or overweight; or changing our accent and the words we use or the stories we tell when we're around "important people," in order to disassociate ourselves from our background or to get ahead in homogeneous workplaces. A few examples tied back to cultural differences include, as someone who is Muslim or follows an Eastern faith, masking that you practice your faith or, even more painfully, removing your articles of faith when you're in public in fear of being labeled "fanatical"; or, as someone who is gay and out at work, self-censoring about your same-gender partner because you worry that your boss will be uncomfortable about your sexuality.

We perform by what we share with the world through social media, choosing carefully the image we present to the virtual world. The curated photos we post might make us look thinner or hotter or younger or happier than we really are; we may comment on, re-post, or "like" life quotes or articles about issues that we actually know or care very little about because "liking" them makes us look like we're "good" people; we may friend/follow/link-in not only with people with whom we have a genuine connection but also with other, random, people so that we look popular.

The main problem with your Performing Self is that it doesn't reflect who you really are, what you're truly feeling, what you're actually thinking, and how you want to behave. It's not authentic.

The more you let your Performing Self win, and the more you bury your Authentic Self beneath it, the more you will feel disconnected, unfulfilled, and powerless.

Many of the people I interviewed shared how painful it has been for them to perform. Indigenous community activist and recent MBA graduate Gabrielle Scrimshaw told me that there were several times when, as a student at a top-notch American university, she conformed and masked her true self in class: "I didn't speak and share as much because I felt like I was struggling to keep up, while my classmates seemed brilliant and I was worried about what they would think." And of course, in not participating in class, Gabrielle's performance and profile were adversely impacted. But then she received an e-mail from a stranger who said, "I'm Native. I've watched your videos. I've never spoken up, but then I saw your stuff. You've been a silent mentor to me." For Gabrielle, it was a moment of "there's a silent majority out there who values what I bring." So she started speaking in class.

In our conversation, activist and educator Dr. Eddie Moore Jr. shared with me that he holds back in how he communicates: "As a Black man, at times I feel some pressure to make people feel safe by always being a 'positive Black man.' I'm often worried about being seen as rude or just feared as a Black man. There are times I pretend to be happy when I'm actually sad or hurting inside; I'm smiling and crying at the same time. I call it 'cryling'— I cry because internally I feel diminished, like I'm losing myself, because I can't be me a hundred percent, while hiding it with a smile." This type of performing has affected Eddie on numerous levels, including manifesting in, as he puts it, "mediocre performance, accomplishments, self-esteem. I feel like I can do my job, but I'm not shining. It's like a personal achievement gap. I'm like a Porsche that can't drive fast ... It feels like fading on the inside." And perhaps the most powerful thing that Eddie said to me is, "When it comes to living authentically, you may be damned if you do, but you'll definitely be doomed if you don't."

While they may be hard to read about, the reflections shared here are extremely insightful on why and how the Performing Self can rear its uncomfortable and painful head. These reflections also highlight the thoughtfulness embodied by people who are committed to living, working, and leading authentically. Not only do they want to live authentically, they make it happen by understanding the triggers that cause them to perform—even if it hurts to do so.

5

What Triggers You to Perform?

If you want to see the face
You must keep the mirror clean
But if the mirror is kept unclean
You cannot see the face therein.

KABIR

NO MATTER how committed we are to practicing authenticity and how hard we try to live and lead authentically as often as possible, we are all bound to lapse into performing at some point. The trigger could be a particular person, issue, situation, environment, behavior, or form of judgment that we believe is coming our way—something about the specific moment causes us to put on the armor of our Performing Self. Triggers typically affect us without us even knowing as they're so deep-rooted.

At the beginning of the last chapter, I told you about my experience sharing my island vacation with the corporate leader and how I was triggered to perform. Through my self-work, I've learned that my key performing triggers tie back to my fear of being judged on the basis of my cultural differences—my race/

ethnoculture and my childhood class/socioeconomic background, and often the intersection of the two—which is exactly what happened with this leader. Now that I know this, when I'm in situations where I feel different because of my race or class (and not in a good way), I'm particularly mindful of whether I'm being authentic and adaptive versus performing.

I've also come to see that our triggers are frequently connected to our experiences and learned behaviors from deep in our pasts, including childhood, that then serve as barriers in our adult lives. The impact of these barriers is profound: they give rise to tendencies to perform that are hard to interrupt because they've become behavioral habits—or, put another way, part of our brain's hardwiring.

The crucial thing for you to figure out is which forces are responsible for triggering you to conform and mask (which we'll do now in this chapter as well as in chapter 6). With this knowledge in hand, you can then train yourself through self-reflection and mindfulness to tune in to and interrupt the effect those forces have on you (which we'll discuss in chapter 7).

Societal Barriers

The overarching force that causes us to perform is the influence of societal norms on our behavior. By societal norms I mean the messages we receive about how to think, feel, and behave through social vehicles like culture, politics, religion, media, the arts, the law, and more.

Over several centuries, philosophers, psychologists, spiritualists, academics, and others have explored the importance of alignment between an individual's actions and societal norms and practices in order to prevent social chaos. These thinkers who have explored social order have it right—societal norms are a necessity in order to keep us functioning effectively as a collective. We need social rules and boundaries to help us live in harmony (and not kill each other, quite frankly). We need help with how to behave, so we learn societal norms about how to act in public and private domains; what to think, feel, believe, and value; how to express our emotions; how to communicate; what to share with others; and how to physically present ourselves. Essentially, societal norms require that individuals alter their behavior—to be their Adapted Selves and even their Performing Selves—in moments when their Authentic Selves would have a significantly adverse impact on others.

At first glance, the issue isn't that society gives us these rules and boundaries for how to behave; the issue is that while societal rules and norms increase social cohesion, they also push behavioral homogeneity and sameness, which help to keep people in check.

Sameness is our comfort zone—we love it! This works well for society, as the more we behave like each other and adhere to the same boundaries, the less social misconduct and discontent there is. We're also wired to seek out behavioral sameness in others. Sameness is easier, faster, and less complicated than difference. We like to force behavioral sameness for all the right reasons, then go overboard with pushing adherence to social rules and boundaries, which includes rigidly enforcing norms even around behaviors that don't have a significantly adverse impact on the collective. So, sameness hurts authenticity.

Many of us get caught up in this hurricane-like push toward behavioral sameness, maybe not noticing that it's impacting our ability to be authentic. In a diverse society or organization, where not everyone is from the same background nor do they share the same values or ideas about accepted behavior, this becomes more complicated still. The pressure mounts to conform and mask in order to make everyone as alike as possible.

For those who are "other" or different from the dominant, majority group, the pressure to conform and mask—to live as the Performing Self—becomes intense. We succumb to this great pressure, in part because of our relentless pursuit of belonging, which you'll remember exploring in the previous chapter.

When we emphasize sameness by encouraging people to downplay their differences, not only do we push them to live less authentically, we also stigmatize differences. Being different becomes bad. People who feel like "others" believe that they will experience negative consequences if they reveal their differences. They fear that they will be judged, face biases, lose opportunities, and—worst of all—have love, acceptance, rewards, and belonging taken away. In this kind of environment, it feels very difficult to be authentic, so you conform and mask your differences. You may also adapt in some situations, which is fine, but it's hard to consistently choose to be your Authentic Self and let your differences shine.

"Covering" is one of the key ways in which we downplay our differences. This term was first put forward by sociologist Erving Goffman in 1963 to describe how even individuals with known, stigmatized identities made a "great effort to keep the stigma from looming large."[1] New York University law professor Kenji Yoshino has significantly developed this concept in his impressive body of work, including a book and an excellent white paper he wrote in partnership with the professional services firm Deloitte entitled *Uncovering Talent: A New Model of Inclusion.*[2] As a fellow inclusion professional, I've seen Kenji present on the topic of covering several times, chatted with him about the link between covering and the push for conformity, and had the pleasure to interview him for this book.

Covering occurs when individuals from stigmatized cultural identities make efforts to de-emphasize their identities. Covering is different than "passing," which takes place when you don't let others know you have an identity characteristic that is stigmatized (for example, a person who has an invisible disability and doesn't reveal that she does). With covering, you disclose that you have the identity that is stigmatized or it's disclosed for you since it can be openly seen (like the color of your skin), but you mute its importance.

In his work, Kenji outlines that there are four axes along which individuals can cover, as follows:

- **Appearance:** altering our self-presentation to blend into the mainstream. Examples: Black women who straighten their hair; a person who takes out a piercing before going in to work.

- **Affiliation:** avoiding behaviors associated with our identity. Example: when Muslims who would otherwise pray during the day choose not to while at work. (Interesting note: affiliation is the axis on which people cover the most, according to Kenji's research, and many of my interviewees shared examples of how they perform with affiliation.)

- **Advocacy:** exhibiting less comfort for "sticking up for" one's group. Example: when a woman doesn't call out a sexist joke in the workplace even though it upsets her.

- **Association:** avoiding contact with other group members. Example: when LGBT professionals choose not to participate in LGBT-focused programming in the workplace—like employee resource or affinity groups—because of fear of attracting bias.

We'll return to the concept of covering when we explore barriers in the workplace (which is a hotbed for performing) in chapter 6.

Family Expectations: The Barriers in High Drive

When I read Don Miguel Ruiz's profound book *The Four Agreements*, I was struck by his words on how children develop their identities. He describes "the domestication of humans" as the process by which humans learn how to live and create their belief systems and, in this context, he explains that children don't have the opportunity to choose their beliefs. Instead they are pushed to agree with the beliefs that are passed on to them by adults (also known as "adultism").

Even when children disagree with adults' beliefs and rebel against these beliefs, children aren't strong enough to win. Ruiz says: "We train our children whom we love so much the same way that we train any domesticated animal: with a system of punishment and reward. We are told, 'You're a good boy,' or 'You're a good girl,' when we do what Mom and Dad want us to do. When we don't, we are 'a bad girl' or 'a bad boy.'" Ruiz goes on to speak of the impact of this powerful system of punishment and reward: children start pretending to be someone they're not in order to please others and because they're afraid of being rejected. In his words, "Eventually we become someone that we are not. We become a copy of Mamma's beliefs, Daddy's beliefs, society's beliefs, and religion's beliefs." [3]

Ruiz's powerful message impressively captures the essence of what I have heard from so many people about the barriers to authenticity and where they learned to perform. In my conversation with Karlyn Percil-Mercieca, a success coach and storyteller, she made the moving comment, "I would like to become more of the little girl who believed she could." Like Karlyn, many of us internalized messages during our childhood about who we "should" be (not who we actually are) and how we "should" behave (not how we want to behave), and this significantly impacts how, and whether, we live, work, and lead authentically as adults.

Parental Pressure as a Barrier

We begin our lives as our true Authentic Selves. As babies, we start off as a blank canvas, with no rules or boundaries for behavior yet imposed, either by ourselves or externally. We are uncensored, uncloaked, and unabashed in how we act. It is on this blank canvas that rules and boundaries for how to behave are written by key caregivers in our lives—our parents, siblings, relatives, teachers, and other elders. Their influence is profound—our parents' influence in particular.

Siblings, relatives, teachers, and other elders may have had a great impact in teaching us how to think, feel, and behave, especially for those of us whose parents' presence was more in the background or those of us who formed strong bonds with elders while growing up. But for most of us, it was our parents who taught, coached, guided, and disciplined us to learn healthy rules and boundaries that would enable us to better function within our families and in society.

For some of us, our parents taught us to access, and live as, our Authentic Self as much as possible. Heidi Levine, a leader at a global law firm, shared with me that her mother encouraged her to live as her Authentic Self. She said her mother did a great job of modeling authentic living as someone who is "very zany, open, and unafraid to be herself." Heidi noted that because her mother is committed to being herself as much as possible, she is consistently joyful ("she farts rainbows and sunshine"), which has inspired Heidi to also live this way.

Sadly, though, many of us didn't have this experience. Instead of learning to radiate our Authentic Selves, we learned to perform. We were bombarded with rigid behavioral rules and boundaries from our parents that pushed us to conform and to mask (for example, messages such as "Don't speak like X, speak like Y," "Don't be friends with/date/marry that person," "Don't study X, study Y"). As Ruiz explained in *The Four Agreements*, our "domestication" was based on a system of rewards and punishments. As we conformed and masked in how we behaved (in other words, when we showed up as our parents wanted us to), we were rewarded with love. When we didn't, we may have been punished and love may have been taken away in certain moments.

In his book *Originals: How Non-Conformists Move the World*, Adam Grant notes that researchers found that from ages two to ten, children are urged by their parents to change their behavior once every six to nine minutes which, as summed up by developmental psychologist Martin Hoffman, "translates to 50 disciplinary encounters a day or over 15,000 a year!" Grant further notes that "when our character is praised, we internalize it as part of our identities... Affirming character appears to have the strongest effect in the critical periods when children are beginning to formulate strong identities."[4]

But for those of us who, rather than receiving praise in our upbringings, primarily received criticism and correction about our character and behavior (picture "You're so insert-X-negative-comment-here-about-who-you-are" or "Stop doing X-authentic-behavior. Instead do Y-performing-behavior"), the effect is to drive the Authentic Self underground and to reward the Performing Self when it shows up, the impact of which can be very challenging to address as we mature. Although being our Authentic Self is what comes naturally at a young age, the love we received during those formative years was often conditional on conforming to our parents' idea of who we should be and how we should behave.

Conditional love, especially from a primary caregiver, leaves deep wounds, pain, and hurt that we carry with us into our adult lives, impacting the extent to which we feel equipped to live, work, and lead authentically. Those of us who grew up feeling intense pressure to mask and conform in our own family feel the impact of this as adults—we find ourselves caught in a cycle of deeply desiring a sense of belonging, but receiving love primarily when we perform, which leads us to continuously perform instead of being authentic, even with those closest to us.

Why did our parents do this? For many of us, our parents were just doing their best based on what they had been taught. They were trying to protect us from the hardships they had experienced and seen, and they wanted to equip us with life tools they believed would help us to live better lives. And, of course, our parents were also nursing their own childhood wounds. This is precisely why I feel such deep love and respect for my parents. I respect their journey and am so grateful for all they have taught me. I have also learned that I can honor them while being honest about the negative impact of some aspects of their parenting.

Many of the people I spoke with revealed the challenges they had with how their parents pushed them to perform. Shakil Choudhury, a leadership consultant and speaker, explained that he learned from his South Asian parents the powerful cultural tradition of putting the needs and feelings of others ahead of one's own. He noted, "The task of always ensuring that others' feelings weren't hurt or de-prioritizing one's own needs meant that saying 'no' was almost impossible to do. The shadow side of extreme empathy and generosity meant another lesson was implicitly taught: if you cannot speak your truth, *lying* is an acceptable alternative."

An area in which I repeatedly heard comments about the effect of parental barriers to living authentically was in career development—and specifically that parents had often laid down inflexible rules about what their children were expected to do to earn a living as adults. My favorite story about resisting our parents' pressure to conform in this area comes from Che Kothari, artist and self-described instigator, because it demonstrates beautifully how being true to your Authentic Self gives rise to art, music, creativity, and culture—which benefits all of us in the world.

In our captivating discussion, Che told me that he struggled with his parents' pressure about how he should earn a living. His parents had moved to Canada from India decades ago with very little money and without being able to fully speak English. They opened a shoe store in a small town, and it was successful and helped his family to prosper.

When Che was around the age of fifteen, his family started visiting the Caribbean. One of the trips was to Curaçao, where it happened to be Carnival. Che had his camera with him, and he jumped into the parade of bands to document it. After that, he was hooked—on photography and Caribbean art and culture. He quickly learned about the power of the camera, and also about cultural gaps that weren't being taught in school. Che felt a deep passion for using photography to share the stories of other cultures, his own and others, and at the age of seventeen he started to call himself a photographer and artist.

When it was time for Che to choose a career, his father told him that he wanted him to go to business school or take over the successful family business, not pursue a career in the arts, which his father deemed to be a hobby. Che told me, "I really struggled [with] my family's pressure about what I should do with my life and how I should live." The struggle was challenging for him, but Che resisted the pressure and decided to pursue his love for the arts because this is what makes his heart sing. He launched a prominent organization, called Manifesto, with the mission of uniting diverse communities of young people through arts and culture. He also cultivated his passion for music, which has led him to now manage prominent artists like the "King of Soca" Machel Montano and to collaborate with many other artists like Chronixx, Protoje, Grammy award winner Angela Hunte, and Mustafa The Poet.

Che continues to resist pressures to conform by, as he puts it, "doing crucial self-development work." Deeply self-reflective, Che continues the yoga practice his parents taught him as a child, meditates as often as possible, and tunes in to his body as a way to experience authenticity. "I also carve out the time to engage in self-reflection—for example, through retreats and travel—and I make sure that I ask myself questions and try to be as present as possible in each scenario... I constantly try to connect with all levels of my self."

I was touched by my conversation with Che. I'm so grateful that he persevered in pursuing his love for the arts because the world is now blessed with his incredible contributions.

Give Your Kids the Gift of Authenticity

Before I leave the subject of the impact of parenting, I would be remiss not to mention that parents have the power to teach their children to flourish as their Authentic Self and their Adapted Self. We push children both to conform and to mask in order to adhere not only to society and others' expectations, but also to adhere to the expectations we impose on them as their caregivers. As a parent, you can be more mindful about how your parenting and conditioning serve as a barrier to your children's authenticity.

When I asked Shakil about how his commitment to living and leading authentically influences how he parents his two young children, he told me that he works really hard to let them be fluid and allow them to be all the parts of their personality. He shared a lovely story about his recent experience giving his four-year-old daughter a bath before bed. He said she was "freaking out" in the tub (misbehaving and not listening) and the last straw was when she took two big gulps of bath water. At his wit's end, Shakil sternly told his daughter, "Enough!" and pulled her out of the tub. And in all of her authentic innocence, she told him, "Daddy, I know I'm a big girl, but I'm also a little girl who doesn't always listen good." Shakil told me that it stopped him in his tracks, as his little girl was reflecting back to him that she has a multiplicity of identities, that she can be all of them, and that she needs him to cultivate this.

Although he admits that he "never feels quite on top of it" (another example of his own authenticity), Shakil says he focuses on giving his kids love for behavior that he may not agree with and gives them choices, asking, "What do you want?" and "How do you want to play?" so that he can be led more by their needs. It sounds like Shakil is laying the foundation for his children to tap into and harness who they are from a young age.

WHILE IT'S often easy to overlook the impact of your childhood experiences on who you now are as an adult ("It was so long ago. Why bother thinking about that?"), when it comes to living authentically, it's imperative to understand the key messages you internalized as a child about being authentic and adaptive versus learning to perform. In exploring how your childhood experiences trigger you to perform, you are peeling back the layers of your experiences, which may be a painful process, but this work is essential to living more authentically and the payoff is great. And remember, you can do this work while simultaneously honoring your caregivers and elders.

Our Peers' Influences as Barriers

While our parents and other caregivers have had a huge impact on how we learned to access our Three Selves, our peers—including our lovers, friends, frenemies, and bullies—have also been there next to us, influencing the extent to which we feel (and felt) comfortable being our Authentic Selves. After our parents and other caregivers, our peers are often the most influential people in our lives—especially in our adolescent and adult years.

They can support us more than anyone, but because of just how important they are in our lives, their negative or limiting behavior can also wound us deeply.

Our lovers include our soul mates, spouses, partners, girlfriends and boyfriends, mistresses and misters, companions, and anyone else we've romanced or who has romanced us. Our friends include our buddies, mates, confidantes, kindred spirits, soul mates, siblings, comrades, and work colleagues. Our frenemies include people who, on the surface, appear to be friends but are actually those who resent, rival, and betray us. (I include them deliberately here because people who engage in these unhealthy behaviors with us are not our true friends despite often being labeled "friends.") And our bullies include those who, through their actions, intimidate, oppress, and harm us, and this may also include anyone in the aforementioned lists of lovers, friends, and frenemies.

Many of us have had wonderful experiences of feeling authentic in the company of our lovers and friends. In their presence we feel safe, loved, and free to be who we are. They encourage us to laugh really loud, wear what we want, share our outlandish views, and love whoever we want to. They create the "container" for us to be safe and authentic. I mean container in the sense of the word as it's used in yoga to describe the energetic space that we create in a physical environment that enables us to relax into the moment, feel trust, and be authentic. (And note, the Authenticity Principle is all about creating the container for us to share with others who we really are, and for others to share with us who they really are—all of which we make happen through our choices and actions.)

But sometimes we also feel pressure from our lovers and friends to perform. If our Authentic Self isn't in alignment with what they perceive to be right, they will either encourage us to adapt our behavior (which is fine) or push us to conform and mask (which is not fine). In fact, even those closest to and most supportive of us can raise barriers to our authenticity without even knowing it and, in some cases, their push to perform is persistent. Our lovers and friends will verbally (e.g., "Umm, you shouldn't do that") and non-verbally (e.g., raising an eyebrow, rolling their eyes, slapping their forehead) signal to you how they think you *should* behave, which may trigger you to perform. And of course, given the deep desire to feel belonging with lovers and friends, the fear of losing love, intimacy, affection, and more causes many of us to significantly conform and mask who we are along the Seven Behavioral Dimensions.

Resisting your peers can be very challenging, but you can stand in your power by consistently choosing to know, embrace, and be who you are. As part of this process, it's important to recognize the signs of those in your peer group who push you to perform rather than support you in being your Authentic Self.

But often it's our frenemies and bullies who influence our behavior in insidious ways that have a far greater negative impact. We're thrown together with them in school, social activities, work, and other situations, and these relationships can be thorny, upsetting, and damaging.

Why do frenemies and bullies have so much power over us? Because they shine a spotlight onto integral aspects of who we are, vilifying these traits and relentlessly reminding us about why they believe we are unworthy and unlovable. Their actions cause wounds and lead us to feel excluded, different, and like "the other." We then carry these wounds around with us, feeling the impact even as adults when someone triggers them inadvertently. We may nurse our wounds whenever we can as grown-ups, in therapy or when a safe container to share has been created by a lover or a friend. But our Performing Self often becomes the armor to protect us from fear, judgment, and hurt.

A very common childhood peer experience that many people carry into adulthood is the trauma of being bullied as a child (the most common forms of which are name-calling, teasing,

and spreading rumors or lies).[5] There is now extensive research
that speaks to the adverse impact of childhood bullying on how
we live as adults, including on our mental and physical health.[6]
Because bullying can have a lasting effect on a child's confidence
and self-worth, you can see how it would have a profound impact
on the ability to be authentic. The scars of childhood bullying
are literally imprinted on your brain and can make it very difficult to embrace your Authentic Self.

It was heartbreaking to listen to story after story in my interviews about how childhood and current-day frenemies and
bullies—made up mostly of (supposed) friends and team members—have hurt people.

Entrepreneur and television personality Bruce Croxon, who
is biracial, disclosed that as a "little Brown guy" growing up in
a White neighborhood, he became aware early on that he was
different and he was certainly made to feel this way. He noted,
"It was too risky to be vulnerable, and so I hid my vulnerability.
My coping mechanism among friends was to be a quick talker,
to be witty." Bruce became good at "verbal jousting," in some
ways to connect with others, but also as a way to deflect the negative attention. These experiences impacted him during his teen
years (he suffered from insomnia and often performed to "fit
in"), which was very hard for him to share back then with others.
Over time, he found empowerment through excelling at sports
and now credits these childhood experiences for his empathy
toward the "against-all-odds underdog."

Remember Drew Dudley, the global leadership speaker who
helped explain the Adapted Self with the teapot analogy? Drew
is smart, fast-talking, funny, and charming (watch his "lollipop
leadership" TED Talk, and you'll see what I mean)—he doesn't
miss a beat, and he's very open to sharing hard-to-discuss
aspects of his life. Drew opened up with me about his painful
experiences with bullying and their impact on his efforts to
become more of his Authentic Self. He told me, "I felt excluded

growing up because I was very chubby and so I always wore sweatpants to school. I had crooked teeth and was called Theodore the Chipmunk. I didn't have the confidence to date and felt like the girls didn't like me … And let me tell you, the kids were so mean. It caused me to overcompensate—I focused on other things to distract the mean kids. I saw myself as an outsider and worked really hard to try to get on the inside."

Drew became an accomplished high school football player, earned the post of president of the student union, and did well academically. But he continued to feel that in order to "fit in" he needed to conform by assuming his peers' identities and personas: "I tried out different things until I wasn't mocked in some way." Explaining why he did this, Drew said, "I think it's human instinct to try to avoid being yourself when you see that 'who you are' is the source of your discomfort. For instance, if you knew that wearing a certain shirt would attract dive-bombing birds every time you walked out the door of your house, you'd go to great lengths to avoid putting on that shirt. Well, imagine that shirt is fundamentally who you are—it's not something that can be removed. You'd do whatever you could to cover it up every time you left the house."

Drew now understands the impact of the bullying he experienced, and he has made great strides in his life to live more authentically. As he told me, "I don't know the secret to happiness, but the secret to unhappiness is when there's a gap between how you conceive of yourself and how you're actually behaving—*and you are aware* of that gap." As a successful leadership speaker, Drew is very open about his life, including his journey with alcoholism and being bipolar, and it's significant to note that Drew told me it's when he talks about this journey in particular that he's most often approached by audience members and told that his story has touched them. Now Drew is proud of being different: "I'd rather be someone's shot of whiskey than everyone's cup of tea."

My own experiences with bullying have also been very revealing to me about my initial challenges with living authentically. It is still incredibly hard for me to think about cutting my hair at the age of fifteen. In the Sikh faith, we do not cut our hair for various reasons, the main ones being that our hair was given to us by the Divine and that our unshorn hair—whether covered by a turban or a scarf, worn in a braid or a bun, or worn loosely—forms part of our personal discipline and unique identity, helping to signal that we are Sikhs. I cut my hair as a teenager not because I no longer believed in my faith or the Divine; I did it so that the taunting would stop, my peers would like me, boys would want to date me, and I would feel a sense of acceptance among the people I had to see at school every day.

Truthfully speaking, this act of conformity did help me with some of my issues—the taunting lessened, more peers seemed to like me, and a few boys did ask me out. And because I got some positive reinforcement for performing, I mistakenly believed that it would bring me joy. But here's the thing: while I had flashes of happiness because I had more moments of social connection, I was never truly accepted into—nor did I feel a sense of belonging in—the social groups to which the doors had opened a crack. While I may have "fit in," I still didn't belong.

Another important point to consider about bullying is that some adults who were bullied as children will, in turn, bully others. One of the leaders I interviewed told me about his realization that after years of experiencing racist bullying as a Black man, he was becoming a bully. He shared a story from his university days when a White student said in his presence, "Can you believe a f*cking n****r won the Super Bowl?" Feeling rage, first he berated the White student and then he locked the student up in a bathroom. He shared with me that as he walked out of the bathroom that day, he realized that in fighting back in this way he was starting to become a bully himself.

As uncomfortable as it is to admit this, my own self-work has revealed that I, too, have bullied others along my path. (Remember, being authentic is about embracing the good, the bad, and the ugly things about ourselves!) I have come to see how, if we don't address the oppression we've experienced head-on and deal with it in healthy ways, we end up bullying and pushing others to conform and mask as well.

THE BARRIERS to authenticity that our peers put up before us have many detrimental effects—they can lead us to feel alienated, wounded, and fearful, which can cause us to alter our behavior to compensate, fit in, and hide who we truly are. At the same time, our peers can also influence and inspire us to be true to who we really are in our interactions.

In a nutshell, our peers—especially our lovers—are critically important to the extent to which we live authentically. The key takeaway here: be sure to choose your closest peers very carefully.

6

The Workplace
Is the Adult Sandbox
for Performing

I've learned that people will forget what you said, people will forget
what you did, but people will never forget how you made them feel.

MAYA ANGELOU

ALTHOUGH MANY of the barriers to living authentically are
created by society and by key people in our lives—parents,
lovers, and other peers—it's in the workplace that adults
experience the greatest push to perform. This is especially the
case when your identity is outside the dominant demographic
that makes up the leadership ranks within your organization.

As adults, it gets easier to avoid family members, break up
with lovers, and un-friend people who expect us to conform to
their way of thinking and acting. But it's exceptionally challenging to escape or challenge leaders and others at our workplace
(let alone the overall organizational culture) who push us to
conform and mask who we are. We have much to risk at work—
our reputation, career trajectory, income—so it's harder to be
vulnerable and courageous in revealing our Authentic Self in a
professional context.

But just because it's harder to do, it doesn't mean we ought to stop trying. Many of us spend most of our time at work, and if this is where we feel forced to be our Performing Self, it will have a significant impact on us. Barriers to authenticity in the workplace are not just exhausting—they can be soul-crushing. It's critical to our well-being that we learn to recognize and break down the barriers so that we can increase our personal, relational, and professional joy.

I mentioned that society pushes behavioral sameness because it is easier, safer, faster, and less complicated than dealing with behavioral differences. Workplaces are a microcosm of society, where a lot of people with numerous differences—be it culture, personality, background, experience, education, learning styles, opinions, or goals—are thrown together and expected to be productive and, usually, to toe the company line. The drive for efficiency encourages organizations to push for sameness through demanding behavioral conformity and masking authenticity.

IMAGINE THAT a workplace is a big sandbox and that everyone in the sandbox has the shared goal of building a huge sand castle. To help with this objective, there are a number of resources in the sandbox (like sand, shovels, buckets, and water) that can be used to build the structure. Everyone in the sandbox has been assigned to a team, has a specific role, and has a leader.

The team leaders want to build the best sand castle possible while maintaining efficiency and cohesion in this tight, shared space. They create formal rules (about how to work, communicate, and socialize), which are enforced rigidly, and over time informal rules also develop. Leaders want team members who will follow the rules—and, in fact, they have conscious and unconscious assumptions about who will do a better job at this—so they actively seek out rule-followers to join the sandbox. They also want rule-following team members who are fun to work with, which means they want to work with people who enjoy socializing in the same ways they themselves do. To make sure rule-following and "fun stuff" happens, leaders will model the behavior required, talk openly about their expectations (either nudging or directing team members to accomplish their tasks), and give out benefits on this basis.

As a team member in the sandbox, if you follow the rules and participate in the fun stuff, you'll be recognized by receiving better work opportunities, guidance on how to do your work, rewards for doing well, and possibilities to grow your role in the sandbox—perhaps you'll even be asked to become a leader yourself. So as a team member, it becomes clear that the more you follow the rules and partake in fun stuff, the better you'll be treated.

For some, following the rules and doing fun stuff naturally aligns with their Authentic Self, so being in the sandbox feels great and they do well. For others, following the rules and doing fun stuff means dancing between their Authentic Self and Adapted Self, but because they're exercising choice in how they behave, it feels good and they, too, are likely to do well. But for others, a lot of the rules and fun stuff feel like undue pressure. It means engaging in a whole lot of performing, doing some adapting, and having very few authentic moments. To them, it feels unnatural, uncomfortable, and exclusionary to be in the sandbox. These team members want to run screaming to find a more inclusive place to work and, frankly, their leaders want them to go too.

Does this sandbox sound familiar? Are you working in this sandbox right now? I suspect that most of you will say yes to at least the first question. That's because this sandbox represents the majority of workplaces. In this sandbox, the organizational culture—and the leaders who reinforce the culture—directly and indirectly push team members both to adapt and to perform.

When some team members feel pressure to conform and mask who they are in order to get ahead, it ties back to a concept called "minimization," an experience wherein people feel pressure to downplay their cultural differences and instead focus on the commonalities they have with the people they're interacting with.[1] Essentially, minimization pushes people to conform and mask in order to advance in their careers.

Minimization Is the Enemy of Authenticity

In my work on inclusive leadership, I leverage a highly effective assessment tool called the Intercultural Development Inventory (IDI) that is used by global organizations across sectors and industries.[2] The IDI measures how culturally competent—or how inclusive—an individual, team, or organization is in working across and adapting to cultural differences. My team and I have now administered the IDI to thousands of people globally, including dozens of leadership teams, in order to help them better understand how inclusive they are of differences in their respective workplaces.

Here's what we have found in leveraging the IDI: the overwhelming majority of organizations (and people) are in the developmental stage of Minimization.[3] And without having tested every person out there, I would argue strongly that our society as a whole is in Minimization.

When an organization is in the development stage of Minimization, this means that while there may be a stated commitment to embracing and leveraging differences, the lived experience is very different. In Minimization, when the "voices of difference" (i.e., people who look and/or behave outside the dominant culture of the leadership) join the organization, the message that they get, essentially, is this: "We love differences. But ... you can look different, but not *too* different. And, more importantly, you need to behave like the rest of us. Be the same!"

Not surprisingly, Minimization has an adverse impact on women, diverse professionals, and anyone else who doesn't behave like the dominant culture that makes up the leadership ranks. For example, an *introverted* older, straight, White, able-bodied Christian male may also feel the sting of minimization in an organizational culture that is all about extroversion.

In Minimization, sameness is the way to get ahead within an organization, and sameness manifests itself in two ways by expecting team members to do the following:

- Behave the same as the leaders → conform (i.e., behave like the extroverted sandbox leader)
- Hide their differences → mask (i.e., hide the fact that they hate the fun stuff the sandbox leader wants to do)

Fundamentally, the message is, *Be your Performing Self!* We feel this reality both in the unspoken and overt messages we receive at work about how to act along the Seven Behavioral Dimensions. The people I interviewed were quick to name this reality in their experiences. Leah Eichler, a business columnist, told me, "Corporations breed conformity. If you want to get ahead, you have to learn quickly about how to adapt. I certainly felt pushed to conform when I worked for a corporation. My preferred way of being is to be collaborative, but I had to pretend to be more direct and dictatorial than I am."

Alice* is a Hong Kong–based lawyer who has worked for a few prestigious firms. In our interview, Alice shared her experiences working in the global business world as an Asian woman. She told me that she often received feedback from one of her former bosses that she needed to be more aggressive in order to impose authority and be successful, including being promoted. (I can

* Not her real name

tell you based on my work that this kind of messaging runs rampant through organizations globally: "Please change who you are to be more [insert-whatever-the-behavioral-expectation-is] to get ahead," even when the behavioral expectation doesn't single-handedly lead to success.) What did Alice do in response to receiving this feedback?

This is what she told me: "I believe in teamwork, collaboration, and cooperation. I wasn't going to start becoming aggressive to people for the sake of being aggressive or getting promoted, because it's not me. For me, being authentic is about being true to yourself, not just in good times but also in times when it may have a less advantageous or less desirable impact on you, especially when you don't share the same philosophy."

Also worth noting is that on the workday I interviewed Alice in Hong Kong, true to her commitment to being authentic, she was rocking a perfectly professional but less conventional outfit than most businesswomen anywhere in the world would be likely to wear to work (think pastel-mauve tweed set instead of a drab black/grey/navy wool suit). Alice told me that in her very conservative profession, her appearance (she always wears a fashionable or professional outfit with a twist) is a small, but meaningful, way she asserts her authenticity and individuality. As we'll discuss in chapter 9, "small stakes" authentic moments help to build the foundation for being more authentic across the Seven Behavioral Dimensions.

Let's go back to the concept of covering and link it to the concept of minimization in the workplace. As discussed in the previous chapter, New York University law professor Kenji Yoshino's comprehensive study of covering in the workplace has revealed some fascinating findings on the prevalence of this behavior. In his research, he found that 61 percent of respondents cover along at least one of the four axes (appearance, affiliation, advocacy, and association) and that 53 percent of respondents feel that their managers expect employees to cover (affirming that minimization is alive and well within workplaces). Kenji's study found that the following demographics reported covering to these extents:

- 83% of lesbian, gay, and bisexual individuals
- 81% of people with a disability
- 79% of Black individuals
- 67% of women of color
- 66% of women
- 63% of Hispanic individuals
- 61% of Asian individuals
- 45% of straight White men

As you would expect, covering has detrimental effects. Respondents in Kenji's study said that covering was "somewhat" to "extremely" detrimental to their sense of self in each axis as follows: 73 percent for association, 68 percent for affiliation, 62 percent for advocacy, and 60 percent for appearance. Showing up as your Performing Self clearly hurts. And as Kenji notes in his research: "Given that everyone has an authentic self, a culture of greater authenticity might benefit all individuals, including the straight White men who have traditionally been left out of the inclusion paradigm."[4]

Let's connect the concept of covering to the Performing Self. When we cover our identity—when we make efforts to downplay our differences or we mute the importance of our identity—we are performing. In doing so, Kenji told me, we strike at our authenticity.

Kenji also shared with me his personal journey with coming out as a gay Asian man and with living more authentically. He said that when he was young, he prayed he would become straight one day and he focused on passing as a straight man. When he eventually came out as a gay man, his focus then was on covering.

A life-changing moment for Kenji happened when he'd just been hired into a prestigious professorship role and a mentor told him after that he'd do much better as a "homosexual professional" rather than a "professional homosexual." His mentor might as well have said, "Don't be you. Advocating for gay rights will harm you. So don't do it." This "advice" lit a fire under Kenji. He vehemently disagreed, pledged to live authentically, and started writing more on gay rights. And like Che Kothari and the many others whose stories I've shared in the book so far, thank heavens Kenji followed his truth, because his work is now making a big impact in many ways and in many places. Kenji explicitly told me, "For those who think that authenticity isn't important, it has changed the course of my life."

On the surface, downplaying our differences at work may appear to help or serve us. But for all of the reasons that I have mentioned, performing actually does more harm than good. Choosing to embrace your differences rather than denying them will change your life.

Disempowerment in the Workplace Sandbox

Within organizational cultures that are in the developmental stage of Minimization, only some people will find that aspects of the culture easily align with their Authentic Self. For example, let's say you are extroverted and a direct communicator, and so the expectation that you build relationships by regularly attending events, by engaging in conversations, by sharing details about yourself, by asking others about themselves, and by speaking at meetings feels comfortable and real to you. But for other people, large aspects of the workplace culture and the related expectations are outside of what is authentic for them. Because of this, they either adapt or perform along the Seven Behavioral Dimensions to meet the expectations.

When you feel comfortable in choosing to adapt your behavior along the dimensions to meet your organization's behavioral expectations in order to get ahead, you're being your Adapted Self. You exercise choice to alter your behavior, you choose to do it to meet your authentic needs or the needs of others, and you feel quite comfortable doing it. Even in situations where you don't love that you're having to adjust, you're still fine with it because you see the benefit from choosing to adapt. For example, even though you might hate public speaking, you'll push yourself to speak more at meetings because your manager has given you feedback that you need to do this to demonstrate you have leadership skills. However, if you're unhappy about changing your behavior, then that's a different story.

You become your Performing Self when you alter your behavior along the dimensions to meet your organization's behavioral expectations, and it doesn't feel right or good. You do it because you see the benefits (you want to get ahead), but it feels uncomfortable, unfulfilling, and exclusionary that you have to do this. You're changing your behavior in a way that is outside your comfort zone—it feels like you're twisting yourself or playing down core elements of who you are, including your differences, to be like your leader and others around you. Eventually you'll feel as though the benefits aren't worth it because you find yourself feeling disconnected, dissatisfied, and disengaged.

Across global workplaces, women in particular continue to be compelled to perform. As Cristina Bonini, a Latin American talent management executive, told me, "In Latin American countries, there continues to be significant masks that people wear at work—especially women. The corporate culture is less formal in some countries than others. But even where it's less formal, there are still high levels of conformity so that you can't speak your mind."

Here are some examples of what women professionals who

work in Minimization cultures have told me about how their Performing Self shows up in the workplace:

- They change their appearance, like their hair, dress, and jewelry, because they worry about looking too womanly, manly, sexy, frumpy, contemporary, conservative, and so on— basically, they feel caught in the double binds of appearance-based bias (damned if you do, doomed if you don't).

- They constantly rethink what they want to say and how they want to say it because they fear that they will be judged as being too timid, bitchy, nasty, indirect, direct, team-oriented, independent, quiet, vocal, and so on—again, they're caught in the double binds of "damned if you do and doomed if you don't," in this case with communication.

- They water down what they share at work about being a mom, afraid that others will think they're more interested in motherhood than career opportunities—so when asked about their weekends, for example, they'll talk about news headlines instead of family stuff.

- They pretend to be interested in sports and may even take up certain sports like golf (ugh, I did that for about twelve days) or read/watch news about sports to "keep up" even though they *hate* it.

- They go to women-hanging-from-poles strip clubs for client- and team-building events. Particularly in the highly male-dominated sectors I consult for, many women professionals have told me that they've gone unwillingly to these places because if they hadn't they would have been the only team member who didn't and therefore would have missed out on spending time with their boss, co-workers, and clients.

Unfortunately, my list of examples of how women conform and mask at work because they feel compelled to by a Minimization culture is much longer than this. Also telling is that I have a similar laundry list of how people from many other identities perform—people of color, immigrants, people from LGBT communities, persons with disabilities, millennials, those who practice religion or a faith (my inclusion work has shown that most workplaces intensely push people who are religiously or spiritually observant to conform and mask), and people from lower socioeconomic backgrounds, to name just a few.

Authentic Voices

What Barriers Do People Experience to Being Authentic at Work?

Many of the people I interviewed shared their experiences with barriers to being authentic at work—barriers caused by minimization that stand in the way of feeling included. Their stories reinforce the pressure to perform and to minimize cultural differences in the workplace, even among senior leaders.

"When I first started to engage the corporate world as an Asian-American, I felt like an outsider because of my ethnicity and lack of educational pedigree . . . I quickly noticed that there were shared experiences and nomenclature that gave others in the 'circle' an edge. It was as if a game was already being played and I showed up too late . . . It still happens now, but I do a far better job of responding to it. I have a new reality—that what I have to offer is of unique value." **Charles Lee**, the CEO of an ideas execution firm and author

"I have so many examples from the corporate world of when I saw people conforming to get ahead, and of course, I did it too . . . I recall a woman who was hired in a senior role. She behaved in a way that reflected that she had taken on a persona of a man to get ahead because this was the way to succeed in a man's world. It was like she was playing a role. I wanted to say, 'You don't have to do that to get ahead.'"

Joyce Roche, a former *Fortune* 500 company executive

"I grew up on the east side of Kansas City. So I often felt different around the posh people in the profession. I was the only African-American junior, and I often felt out of place because of my class and race differences, and I often hid my class background because I felt insecure. It was hard to be myself... I finally shared my story with my colleagues about living in a neighborhood where I heard gunfire the night before, and they were shocked."

Michelle Wimes, a professional development leader

The reality for many women, diverse professionals, and others who are different (whatever those differences are) is that they'll likely perform at work in many of the Seven Behavioral Dimensions, they'll adapt in others, and they'll be authentic in just a few, if any. If you can relate to this, you know how draining and disillusioning this feels. As I have been told again and again, it is "exhausting" to feel left out, to be not included for who you are, and to be someone you're not while at work. You can now see why I refer to minimization as the enemy of, and the biggest barrier to, authenticity (and inclusion) in the workplace.

While leaders and inclusion professionals work hard to shift workplace cultures, in the meantime you still need to earn a living within environments where you likely want to not just survive but thrive. The Authenticity Principle offers you a framework that will enable you to better check in with yourself so you can understand how you want to behave and potentially adjust in workplaces that are evolving. I'll address the question of "When should I be authentic versus adaptive at work, and what do I about the expectation to perform at work?" in chapters 8 and 9. If you're a leader and wondering how to interrupt minimization in the workplace, you'll find a range of strategies in chapter 10.

Now we'll do a deep dive into exploring how we can move away from performing by focusing on doing the critical self-work that is needed to embrace who we are. Without embracing who we are, we'll never be able to live, work, and lead authentically, which is what makes it such a vital part of our journey in practicing authenticity.

7

Embrace Who You Are and Stop Performing

Where there is love, there is no fear.

GURMUKH KAUR KHALSA

YEARS AGO, I was invited to an event exclusively for women in leadership. I was excited to go—it was a great chance to network with accomplished women, be inspired, and spread the word about the work that I was doing. But I was also nervous about going—you know the feeling you get when you walk into a room of complete strangers and have to force yourself not to get glued to the cheese table.

Upon arriving, I quickly noticed that the "who's who" of senior businesswomen were there and that I was one of the few younger people and women of color in attendance. I didn't recognize anyone and I found myself having to make a real effort to insert myself into conversations. It already felt pretty awkward, but it got even more uncomfortable when I noticed that several of the women I introduced myself to would look at my name tag and then survey the room over my shoulder while I spoke. As this continued to happen, I could feel myself getting more and more tense. At the time, I didn't know it, but my Performing Self was there in full effect: I was spending a lot of time self-silencing, sporting a put-on laugh and perma-smile, and when I did speak it was in an annoying high-pitched voice.

The breaking point came when I decided to approach a woman who had just left a conversation and was standing alone (because this is what we learn in "how to network" workshops). I walked toward the woman slowly with a big smile on my face and she made eye contact with me. As she smiled back and her eyes darted to my name tag, she turned her body in a different direction and then started to walk away.

I felt crushed. My heart was pounding, my mind was racing, and I could feel myself getting hot—all of which signals to me that I'm about to cry. As I took a deep breath to calm myself, I heard The Voice in my head say two significant things. The first was, "You never have to come to this event again." (And FYI, I have not gone back despite being invited back repeatedly.) And the second, more significant, thing The Voice said was—and it shocked me even as I heard it—"One day when I'm important, when I'm somebody, they'll take me seriously."

For days afterward I reflected on the deeper meaning of those words. It became increasingly clear to me that despite all my personal, academic, and professional strengths, accomplishments, and awards and distinctions, there was something about that event that had led me to feel insignificant in my skin. I felt like I wasn't enough next to those women. I felt as though I needed external validation in order to belong and to be accepted. My self-limiting beliefs were causing me to self-silence, to hide who I am, and to change my behavior in ways that I didn't actually want to.

The experience opened up my eyes to a few realizations: I was continuing to carry around with me a number of self-limiting beliefs; these beliefs were untrue stories that I was telling myself; these untrue stories were causing me to perform; and the result was that I was suffering.

In response, I kicked up the work I was doing to embrace myself—the authentic me. This self-work was instrumental to cultivating the self-love that I needed in order to live more authentically and to experience more joy. In this chapter, I share with you practices for embracing who you are from my own personal experiences and from my work with others.

I TEACH the concept of "self-empowered leadership," which is the idea that we must take ownership of managing and leading ourselves as individuals in addition to relying on others to help support us. Essentially, self-empowered leadership is rooted in the concept that you must "own your own shit" in order to increase your joy. It's unconstructive to fault the external world entirely for why you're not being supported. It's not enough (or even healthy) to only look to others for support; you must support yourself as well.

Sometimes when I put this concept out there, I get pushback from people who will say, "In a society or workplace with entrenched systemic barriers and obstacles, aren't you blaming 'the victim' when you say that we need to take responsibility for ourselves, for what happens to us?" My response is unequivocal: I'm deeply committed to helping to create a world where every one of us feels empowered and included. I'm all about dismantling the system that holds some of us back while propelling others forward (hence why I spend so much time teaching inclusion to senior leaders).

But! We co-create what happens to us. As part of this co-creation process, we each must be accountable and take responsibility for our own role in what happens to us. This means that you must examine the external barriers that are getting in the way of you living authentically as well as examine what you're doing that's getting in your own way. What I'm referring to are your self-limiting barriers—untrue beliefs that you have about yourself or tell yourself, which you then reinforce through your behavior, both knowingly and unknowingly.

The good news is that you can also use your behavior to interrupt and dismantle these barriers. You have the power and ability to change your behavior and alter your experiences through the choices you make, even through tiny choices that initially feel insignificant. The starting point is to focus on fully accepting—*embracing*—who you truly are (remember: the good, the bad, and the ugly).

In this chapter, we'll look at how you can better embrace who you are by identifying and interrupting the self-limiting beliefs and barriers that are holding you back from accepting yourself and from living more authentically. We'll focus on how to engage in behavioral change by delving further into what causes you to live as your Performing Self, why that's happening, and how you can address it. In particular, we'll focus on how to push yourself away from performing and more toward being adaptive and authentic along the Three Selves continuum by exploring the following key strategies:

- Recognize when you're performing.
- Identify your internalized biases.
- Disrupt your negative narratives.

Using these strategies for behavioral change will help you to directly identify, interrupt, and address the reasons why you're performing rather than being authentic, thereby helping you to reveal the work that you must do to overcome your obstacles and live more authentically.

Peeling the Layers

In learning to embrace yourself, the self-work you'll do will ultimately help you to cultivate self-love (unconditional acceptance of yourself) and self-compassion (treating yourself with the same kindness with which you'd treat others), both of which are essential for practicing authenticity. It'll be like you're peeling the layers of an onion to get to the root of why you feel afraid, vulnerable, imperfect, unworthy, angry, sad, and/or inadequate. It means going through a process of learning about how to heal your wounds and your broken-heartedness in order to cultivate unconditional self-acceptance and self-love.

While this may sound easy, it's usually not. It requires that you immerse yourself in the tough, gritty self-work of soul-searching and exposing your own inner demons. It's work that will make you cry, scream, laugh, and feel nauseous. It means exploring your personal history and certain situations that cause you to feel despair. This is all *very* hard work.

I call this not just hard work, but "heart work." I deliberately refer to the heart because the heart is all about courage and love, and we need both to do the heavy lifting—the self-work that's at the core of the Authenticity Principle. We need courage because it takes strength, perseverance, and guts to face the challenges that come with learning to accept and embrace who we are. And we need self-love because our wounds and broken hearts hurt, and the cure to this hurt is love. Self-love plays an incredible role in healing and empowering us to be more authentic. Even in the face of judgment, with self-love we can courageously embrace and be who we are. This work may feel "soft" and "mushy" for some of you—and it is—but it also takes a tremendous amount of courage.

Hand in hand with self-love is self-compassion. Perhaps the foremost expert in the study of self-compassion is Dr. Kristin Neff, a professor of education at the University of Texas at Austin. Dr. Neff explains that self-compassion is the kindness and care you'd give to yourself like you would give kindness and care to a friend. She notes that self-compassion allows for greater self-clarity because it allows us to acknowledge our flaws, challenges, and insecurities with kindness and, as such, we don't feel the need to hide them or push them down.[1] Practicing self-compassion will help you to explore your self-limiting barriers, beliefs, and behaviors: what they are, why you have them, how they cause you to conform and mask, and how to interrupt them in a non-judgmental way. The kindness and care you direct at yourself will enable you to be more patient, open, and tender. As a result, you'll do a better job of disrupting your self-limiting beliefs and behaviors, and in turn you will be less inclined to conform and mask.

If you're wondering what self-compassion looks like in the context of practicing authenticity, consider an example from Chris Miller, an inclusion professional, who shared with me that one of his key self-compassion practices is to pay attention to when he engages in self-flogging (a.k.a. self-criticism). The specific practice Chris leverages is monitoring how he speaks to himself. He will proactively interrupt the use of language like "I should do this" or "I must do this"—language that is laden with judgment and the pressure to perform—and replace it with "I want to do this," reminding himself of his behavioral motivators/drivers. Interestingly, in my interview with Jai-Jagdeesh, the celebrated musician and yogi who I mentioned earlier, she gave the exact same example of how she practices self-compassion.

Since hearing both Chris and Jai-Jagdeesh offer this as a strategy, I've been attempting to minimize my use of the words "should" and "must" and ramp up my use of language like "I want to" and "It would be helpful to" and "I'll enjoy." Here's what I can tell you: It's hard to do because "should" and "must" are so entrenched in how we speak to ourselves and to others. But the impact of using the other language I mentioned is much less pressuring and much more motivating, which makes it worth the effort.

In a nutshell, engaging in both self-love and self-compassion will be fundamental in your difficult journey from performing to being more adaptive and authentic.

Recognize When You're Performing

In order to show up more as your Authentic Self or, at minimum, your Adapted Self, you must first understand when you're performing to fit in. The central questions for you to reflect upon in depth are: (1) In what situations are you performing, (2) In which behavioral dimensions are you performing, and (3) Why?

Your answers to these questions are likely to be highly illuminating, as they'll reveal places deep within where you feel wounded, insecure, vulnerable, afraid, judged, ashamed, unworthy, angry, and more. Your answers will also reveal the areas in your life where you feel like you don't have the *choice* to behave in ways you want to and where you feel pressure to be someone you're really not—and, as we've already discussed, being able to exercise choice is critical for living authentically.

As you dig into these three questions, you'll also have the opportunity to explore the barriers that are in your way for cultivating self-love and self-compassion. You'll start to get a better feel for what The Voice is telling you about why you ought to conform and mask, what is wrong with you and your differences, and why you "shouldn't" reveal yourself to others. These types of insights will speak directly to the obstacles that are likely blocking you from cultivating self-love and self-compassion.

Now we'll take a moment for you to reflect on what is causing you to perform and how your Performing Self shows up.

Reflection Moment

- **A Deep Dive into the Seven Behavioral Dimensions**
  (See pages 23–4 for the detailed description of the dimensions.)
  In which of the following Seven Behavioral Dimensions do you
  perform? How do you conform or mask? Why is this happening?
  - in how you express your emotions
  - in how you communicate non-verbally
  - in the words you use when you speak
  - in how you speak
  - in the content you share
  - in your actions
  - in how you dress/appear

The Effect of Life Experiences on Performing
- What three experiences (relational or work) have compelled you
  to perform?
- What is it about these experiences that caused you to perform?
- What will you do going forward to address the impact of these
  experiences on your current behavior?

Authentic Living Insight
Do You Have an "Elephant Story"?

In her work, Karlyn Percil-Mercieca, a success coach and storyteller,
describes a concept she calls the "Elephant Story."

As Karlyn explains, an Elephant Story is a shame- or fear-based
experience in your life, often from your childhood and/or culture,
that you haven't addressed. It's like the elephant in the room—it's
huge, you know it's there, but you don't address it because the process is painful (it feels like Pandora's box). And because you haven't
addressed its impact, your Elephant Story blocks the pathway to
living, loving, and leading in a joyful way.

Karlyn openly shares that one of her Elephant Stories was the years of childhood sexual assault she experienced by a relative, and how she didn't acknowledge to anyone—including herself—that she'd had this experience until she was in her mid-twenties. But the impact was undeniably there: she "kept people out," built a wall around her heart, and didn't believe she was worthy of love or happiness. It was only when she acknowledged, owned, and then began to work through her Elephant Story that she learned to love herself, take more risks, and raise her hands for opportunities.

In our interview, Karlyn connected the Elephant Story with living, working, and leading authentically. She told me that because our Elephant Story is part of who we are, if we don't acknowledge the experience and the adverse impact it may be having on how we live, it may block the pathway to our Authentic Self. More importantly, we may end up conforming and/or masking to hide the experience from ourselves and others. This doesn't mean that we need to tell everyone, or even anyone, about the experience, but we benefit from addressing the experience on a personal level. In doing so, it helps us to rewrite the story in a way that serves us.

Other people I interviewed also shared the impact of a particular life experience on their ability to live, work, and lead authentically. Sonya Kunkel, the chief inclusion officer and vice president of people strategies at a global bank, told me that she learned over time about how to share her story of growing up as a foster child: "We need to be true to our stories. We have a choice on what we share and how we share . . . I now share my story. People don't necessarily treat me differently—but they become much more open with me."

For Dr. Eddie Moore Jr., who's an activist and educator, his experiences with addiction caused him to cover up his low self-esteem and his fear of failure, both of which were preventing him from understanding who he really is. In our interview, he spoke of how his journey of getting clean—"doing his work"—uncovered his

Authentic Self: "When I stopped drinking and doing drugs, my journey of cleaning up uncovered who I really am." I asked him what was revealed to him once he became clean and Eddie boldly replied, "That I'm audacious, capable of anything I put my mind to . . . I gave up the belief that I always need to have a boss. It was liberating to have freedom. I felt like, 'I can f*cking do this.' I now dream big, think big. I don't shoot for clouds. I'm going for the stratosphere." Bam!

Reflection Moment

- What is your Elephant Story or pivotal life experience that you've pushed deep down and haven't yet addressed? Why?
- How is it impacting the ways in which you conform and/or mask who you are?
- What can you do to address it going forward?

Identify Your Internalized Biases

Our internalized biases can trigger us to perform. For example, talent management leader Lori Lorenzo told me she didn't want to tell anyone about her divorce when it first happened many years ago, "because I felt like a failure at building a relationship, like I wasn't a good parent (because you shouldn't get divorced), like I wasn't going to be a good worker (because as a single parent it's hard to juggle both parenting and a job)." In an effort to hide the burden of the changes in her personal life, Lori performed. Not only was it emotionally draining and not authentic, it alienated some of her colleagues and it impacted her ability to build relationships she critically needed during that time.

A few years later, when navigating the special needs diagnosis for all three of her sons, Lori knew from her earlier experience performing after her divorce that she needed to be authentic in order to build and preserve relationships that would carry her through another difficult time: "I had to reframe everything and share openly about the experience. This required vulnerability, but the resulting authenticity drew people toward me, and those who were able to rallied around me."

In my inclusion work, I teach extensively on implicit bias, the unconscious mental shortcuts our brains take in making decisions about people who are different than us, the people we put in our "outgroups" (a term used to describe a group of people we don't identify with, usually because they don't share our identities). I use a framework I've developed for understanding bias, which identifies three key things that happen with bias as it relates to differences:

1   **We dish it out:** Everyone engages in biased behavior directed at others. For example, research shows that the overwhelming majority of us have preferences for light-skinned people over dark-skinned people (in other words, White people over people of color).[2] Another example is something I call "meetings bias": when at a meeting a woman offers an insight that isn't acknowledged, and then five minutes later a man makes the same comment and the room erupts into thunderous praise—even though *she* said the same darn thing five minutes prior.

2   **We receive it:** Conversely, everyone is on the receiving end of others' biases. For example, people sometimes walk into a room where I'm presenting and they pre-judge that the session will be lousy or subpar just because I'm a young-looking Brown girl. I know this because sometimes leaders come up to me the end of a session and say, "When you first started to speak, I thought, 'This is going to be a waste of my time,' but wow, did I ever learn a lot today!" Yup, this actually happens.

3 **We internalize it:** Many of us (but not all, which is important to note) internalize the biases coming our way about our identities, which essentially means that we knowingly and unknowingly hold the negative messaging directed at our identities. For example, significant biases continue to be directed at people who live with mental health conditions, including there being uncertainty about their competence. I've heard from numerous people who live with anxiety and depression who would be excellent candidates for promotions within their organizations, but they don't put their names forward because they question their own abilities due to the negative messaging they've internalized.

I am particularly fascinated by the third aspect of bias—that some of us internalize the biases that come our way about our identity—for these three reasons: (1) I have lived this and have seen firsthand how it's held me back in experiencing joy in all areas of my life, (2) it's under-discussed, and (3) it's highly prevalent among women and diverse people in particular.

With internalized bias, we absorb the biases, stereotypes, assumptions, judgments, and hatred about our identities, and then we knowingly and unknowingly act out what we've absorbed. (You may have also heard this referred to as "internalized racism, sexism, homophobia, or X-ism.") In other words, we *believe* the negative messaging that comes our way about who we are. And because there's more negative messaging about certain identities than others (for example, people of color over White people, women over men, overweight people over thin people), some of us are inclined to internalize negative messages much more than others.

In the context of the Authenticity Principle, when we internalize biases, our "Who I am markers" are impacted by the negative messages others are sending our way about our identity. The negative messages become so much a part of us that we turn them into negative self-talk, believing them to be true and being guided by them rather than being guided by the voice of our Authentic Self. And even if we don't believe the negative messaging, it can still adversely impact us because we may feel pressure to defend or shield against it. This will likely cause an agitated stress response in our body and deplete mental energy, leading to underperformance. All of this causes us to suffer as a result. It literally hurts our minds, souls, and bodies.[3]

I often present on leadership and empowerment to women and diverse people, and during my presentations I will explore the audience members' experiences with internalized biases. I'll ask a question that sounds something like "How many of you have ever told yourself, 'Don't speak or challenge this person or raise your hand for this opportunity,' because as a woman, person of color, [insert-the-difference], you feel less worthy?" Sadly, at least 75 percent of my audiences put their hands up. And, by the way, this is conscious awareness; that is, in these cases attendees are aware of their internalized biases—they've actually heard The Voice say these negative things. Imagine the negative messaging being said in their unconscious minds that they're unaware of.

If what I'm telling you sounds implausible, consider the findings from the Implicit Association Test (IAT), which is administered through an organization called Project Implicit.[4] The IAT is a free, confidential, online tool that can be used to determine what your unconscious associations are for certain identities. There are several tests within the IAT, and my favorite tests to use with my audiences are the Gender-Career IAT (to determine bias against women) and the Skin Tone IAT or Race IAT (to determine racial bias—it was the Skin Tone IAT research results I was speaking of earlier, under "We dish it out"). The

IAT and Project Implicit's work are extremely impactful—they help to make nay-saying executives sit up and listen during my unconscious bias presentations, and it gives me the credibility to shield against the biases I'm up against.

Here are some findings from the work around the IAT that relate to internalized bias:

- On the Gender-Career IAT, about 75 percent of respondents associate "male" with "careers," and "female" with "family," and interestingly, 80 percent of women respondents have this association. This means that these women also unconsciously connect men with careers and women with families.[5]

- On the Race IAT, which measures people's unconscious associations for Black people and White people, almost 75 percent of those who take the IAT on the Internet or in laboratory studies reveal an automatic preference for White people, and almost 50 percent of the Black people who have taken this IAT also have an automatic preference for White people over Black people. Project Implicit explains: "Data collected from this website consistently reveal approximately even numbers of Black respondents showing a pro-White bias as show a pro-Black bias. Part of this might be understood as Black respondents experiencing the similar negative associations about their group from experience in their cultural environments, and also experiencing competing positive associations about their group based on their own group membership and that of close relations."[6]

A key message here from the IAT research is this: we can be biased against our own identities. This happens because we internalize the negative messaging that comes our way about the groups we belong to and, therefore, who we are.

How do we internalize biases? Back to the brain and neuroscience. As you take in data from your external environment, your brain will categorize and store the data, including the associations and messaging you are exposed to. So, your brain will see a person with a particular identity (e.g., a Hispanic woman), and whatever associations and messaging you are being given at the time about that person (e.g., analytically inferior, feisty, overly emotional—highly common, negative stereotypes about Hispanic women in society today), your brain will store that information along with the person's identity. Your associations are then reinforced the more you're exposed to similar messaging about the particular identity—even when you belong to that cultural group.

Because we often take in essentially the same messages about our cultural identities as others, we, too, will store the negative messages about our own identities in our brain. We *internalize* the negative messages.

When we internalize biases about our identities, it leads us to doubt, censor, and disparage ourselves. We feel bad about who we are, which impacts how we behave—both consciously and unconsciously: we downplay what makes us different (the basis for the bias), we feel inferior (more on this in the next section about the impostor syndrome), we feel unworthy, and so we often conform and mask who we are. This chain reaction impacts our ability to be our Authentic Self and even our Adapted Self.

Many of us—especially those of us who come from underrepresented and marginalized cultural communities—have both knowingly and unknowingly come to believe the negative messaging that comes our way from others about who we are, and especially about what makes us different. We feel like the "other" because our differences are mischaracterized, misunderstood, and devalued. These messages become so much a part of us that we believe them to be true and are guided by them, rather than being guided by our Authentic Self. Because of our feelings of otherness and unworthiness, we downplay our differences and perform to fit in.

So what can you do to interrupt this destructive cycle? You first want to figure out which biases and messages you've internalized and what their impact is; and then challenge their validity by replacing them with positive, healthy beliefs about who you are (which we'll discuss in the upcoming section on negative narratives). To identify your internalized biases, here are some tools and strategies you can leverage:

Take the Implicit Association Test

There are several tests within the IAT and you can take as many of them as you like to determine if you hold biases about your own cultural identities. Once you have taken the IAT, consider the following:

- What did the IAT reveal about your internalized biases?

- Upon reflecting on your IAT results,
  - what negative messages have you internalized about your cultural identities?
  - what is the impact of this?

Explore the Impact of Internalized Bias

To help you interrupt the biases and messaging you've internalized, you'll want to explore the impact of your experiences with performing, exclusion, and otherness. To assist you with this, answer the following questions as candidly as you can:

- What are the negative messages and forms of bias that have come your way based on your identities? To what extent do you believe these negative messages and forms of bias are true?

- What is the impact of bias, exclusion, and otherness on
  - your behavior?
  - how you feel about yourself?
  - how you perform (conform or mask)?

Disrupt Your Negative Narratives

Years ago, when I completed my leadership coaching certification in neuroscience-focused strategies, we explored the silent traps in our brain that are based on untrue stories we tell ourselves *about ourselves* and that cause us to hold back or shut down in certain situations. I refer to these as our "negative narratives." These negative narratives are self-limiting beliefs that we hold (they may reflect the biases we've absorbed); they loop in our heads knowingly and unknowingly; and their impact is profound. Because our negative narratives make us feel bad about ourselves or that something is wrong with us, they translate into a whole lot of conforming and masking of who we are rather than living authentically.

For example, one of my own negative narratives was revealed in my story earlier in this chapter about the women's leadership event. I believed I was being shunned because I look young, am a woman of color, and was junior in seniority compared to the more established businesswomen. This feeling of being shunned triggered my insecurities and pre-existing question marks about my worthiness, which are tied back to the biases I've internalized. Somewhere deep inside me, my narrative was that I'm not good enough because I wasn't "important" or a "somebody" yet, and so it made sense to me that I was being snubbed. I felt like an impostor.

Perhaps you can relate to my story because you've had similar experiences. Consider whether you've had moments when you felt any of the following:

- Your success is due to luck.
- Others will discover that you lack certain abilities.
- You're doubtful about repeating your successes.
- You won't be able to live up to expectations.
- Everyone around you is far more intelligent/capable.

If these types of feelings are common for you, you may have the "impostor syndrome," as it's commonly known (it's also referred to as the "impostor phenomenon")—constant feelings of inadequacy and self-doubt about your abilities despite external evidence of your competence. Our understanding of impostor syndrome is largely based on the work of clinical psychologist and professor Dr. Pauline Rose Clance, in collaboration with clinical psychologist Dr. Suzanne Imes. (The self-reflection bullets above are adapted from Dr. Clance's test for determining if you have the impostor syndrome.[7]) Dr. Clance's work reveals that when we feel like impostors, we feel like frauds who are going to be "found out." We are racked by our negative narratives that reflect our fears, insecurities, and vulnerabilities, which we go to great lengths to mask so that we appear stronger or more confident than we actually are. We hope it will throw others off—that they won't see that we're afraid or hurting—while feeling panicked that we'll be exposed.

We often hear about the impostor syndrome in the context of exploring the experiences of women, but it impacts men as well. In fact, based on my work with leaders across different backgrounds, I have found that most people have experienced the impostor syndrome in some way. This is also what the research says—that impostorism is found around the world across ages, races/ethnocultures, professions, and experiences.[8]

For example, entrepreneur and television personality Bruce Croxon (who is highly successful by many measures) shared with me that he used to be affected by the impostor syndrome and is now comfortable with openly talking about this. He told me, "I was impacted by the impostor syndrome early on in my investing career because I would invest in people's ideas, thinking that 'if a guy like me could make an idea work, then surely you must be able to.' It was obviously a lack of confidence and acknowledgement on how hard it was to achieve what I had."

I had the pleasure of interviewing Joyce Roche, a highly accomplished former executive in the beauty industry and, notably, the first African-American woman officer of a *Fortune* 500 company. Joyce is also the former CEO and president of Girls Inc. and the author of *The Empress Has No Clothes*, a best-selling book about impostor syndrome. She shared with me that she came from humble beginnings (her mom was a domestic worker) and that she was one of few women, and even fewer women of color, when she attended Columbia Business School decades ago. Joyce gave me her insights on the connection between the impostor syndrome and living authentically: "The impostor syndrome is hugely linked to authenticity because it causes you to hide portions of who you are, because you question whether you're good enough or acceptable enough." Looking back at her younger self, she can now see how the impostor syndrome affected her: "Outwardly, I looked confident and in control, but internally it was very different because I had all kinds of negative messages going through my head about my abilities. Every time I took on something new, I would feel fear. I asked myself, 'Can I compete, will I be acceptable, will I succeed?'"

In writing her book, Joyce had the opportunity to tease out her experiences with the impostor syndrome with Dr. Clance and, in doing so, was able to see that she had these feelings of inadequacy partly because she was immersed in environments where most people were not like her. Not only did Joyce feel like she had to work harder, she felt like she had to hide her differences and keep a large part of herself "under wraps." She told me that she constantly wondered, "Are they going to accept me even though I'm different?"

Joyce's feelings of being an impostor caused her to perform—to mask, in particular. For example, because she was now competing with many White men who grew up affluent, she didn't feel comfortable talking about her family and humble upbringing. She would divert by letting people talk about themselves. She also altered her speech to sound more formal and would often hear, "She's so articulate." (FYI, this language raises a "bias flag" when used in reference to people of color.) She dressed significantly more conservatively than she wanted to. On this note, Joyce shared with me an example of a colleague—a White woman executive—who often dressed "outside the box" (e.g., wearing cowboy boots to work). But Joyce told me, "As a minority woman, it was hard to stand out in that way... I didn't want to do anything that would cause the spotlight to shift off my performance."

Toward the end of our conversation, when I asked Joyce what her sixty-eight-year-old self would tell her younger self, she replied, "While I wouldn't change a thing, I wish I had been more comfortable about who I was. I'd tell her that."

Words to live by! So many of us are caught up in The Voice's negative loop that tells us all kinds of wrongness: "You're not capable. Your success is a fluke. You're not smart enough." Our feelings of being an impostor impede us from being authentic because we hold back who we are.

Let's go back to my experience at the women's event. It was illuminating because it caused me to pay more attention to the self-limiting narratives I was consistently playing in my head, most of which connected back to internalized bias. Essentially I started to tune in much more often to what I was saying to myself *about myself*. Through my self-work (regular therapy, meditation, self-care routines, mindfulness retreats, and tons of self-study), I started to question my negative narratives and replace them with positive affirmations about who I am. So now when I go to an event where people don't speak to me as much or their eyes dart away from me, I don't take this as personally (I tell myself, "Their behavior isn't about you"). I don't know what their behavior is about (they could be having a bad day), but it doesn't matter as much to me because I increasingly know my worth.

So what can you do to interrupt your negative narratives, be they connected to internalized bias, the impostor syndrome, or otherwise? Here are a few key strategies:

Figure Out What Your Negative Narratives Are

Before you can work to disrupt them, you need to start off by figuring out what your negative narratives are. Or, in other words, what does The Voice tell you about yourself? This is a tough reflection for most of us because, for one thing, we don't routinely look for this. Also, our minds are often so active and filled with noise that we can't even hear The Voice (mindfulness practices to the rescue!).

Here are some self-reflection questions that you can use to help you better understand what your negative narratives are and their impact:

- When you tune in to The Voice, what are the top three negative narratives you hear it saying about yourself?

- For each of those negative narratives, complete the following:
  - Where did this narrative come from, or how did it come to be?
  - I keep telling myself this narrative because…
  - I know that this narrative is untrue because…
  - A positive belief that I can replace this narrative with is…

Challenge, Don't Dismiss Your Negative Narratives

Neuroscience tells us that when we dismiss a thought by telling ourselves, "Oh, that's a bad thought—don't think that," the thought will then loop in our unconscious mind in a phenomenon called "ironic rebound effect." Suppressing beliefs, thoughts, or emotions can cause them to return even stronger than before, which can have a negative effect on well-being.[9] Going forward, when you hear The Voice utter a negative narrative, negative self-talk, or a self-limiting belief, rather than pushing the thought away, explore it and process it. You can do this by questioning what you've heard yourself say. Ask yourself:

- Is this true?
- What is a positive, more accurate narrative that I can tell myself?

Create New Thoughts to Replace Negative Narratives

In her fascinating book, *My Stroke of Insight*, Harvard Medical School neuroanatomist and professor Dr. Jill Bolte Taylor (who also has an incredible TED Talk) chronicles her experience with a severe hemorrhage in the left hemisphere of her brain, which impacted her ability to walk, talk, read, write, and recall any of her life. It took eight years for Taylor to recover her physical function and thinking ability.[10]

She poignantly describes how she controls negative self-talk by consciously creating new thoughts (controls generating new brain circuits that make it difficult for pre-existing negative circuits to monopolize her mind).[11] To replace a negative comment (narrative), she will instead focus on something she finds fascinating that she'd like to ponder more deeply, think about something that brings her terrific joy, or think about something she would like to do. Similarly, other experts will tell you to replace your negative self-talk with positive affirmations or truths about yourself.

With this in mind, going forward, when confronted with a negative narrative, what are three things that you can

- think about that bring you great joy?
- reflect on that you find fascinating?
- tell yourself repeatedly that make you feel good inside?

Authentic Living Insight
Engage an Expert

Sometimes the help we need we can't give to ourselves (we've tried the strategies mentioned in this book and more, but they're not helping us), and instead we need to engage an expert to get it. If this is the case for you, I encourage you to consider working with an expert (such as a psychotherapist, life coach, or body-work therapist). Many of the people I interviewed told me that experts helped them identify, understand, and address their self-limiting beliefs and behaviors, and helped them to do the really deep work of cultivating self-love and self-compassion.

I recognize that this will be cost-prohibitive for some, and I empathize with that (it was challenging for me to pay for experts in my early twenties when I first started my therapy work). But if you can stretch to make it happen, it could be one of the best investments you ever make in your personal and professional growth. As I know from personal experience, when you're working with the right person, it's worth every penny. So my hope is that for those who are interested in seriously pursuing the path of authenticity, you are able to find the resources at some point to make this happen if you need it. And if this is outside your reach at this moment, all is not lost. There are a wealth of resources to help you, including books, online reference materials like videos and podcasts, and other self- and group-guided strategies, practices, and tools that you can leverage.

Going forward, recognize when you need external help with your authenticity journey, and seek it out when you do.

LIVING MORE authentically can happen only when you do the deep self-work and heart work to embrace who you are. You must be willing to acknowledge the difficult, even traumatic, experiences you've had in your life; the less-than-desirable behavior you engage in; and the negative messages you regularly send to yourself about yourself. Only then will you be able to create the behavioral change needed for you to live as your Authentic Self and your Adapted Self.

We'll now focus on exploring your Adapted Self—what it means to be adaptive, why this is a critical place along the Three Selves continuum, and how to be adaptive.

8

Your Adapted Self: Meeting Your Needs and Others' Needs

There is no passion to be found playing small—in settling for a
life that is less than the one you are capable of living.

NELSON MANDELA

ONE OF the people I had the pleasure of interviewing for this book is Alex Kopelman, who is the co-founder, president, and CEO of the American non-profit organization Children's Arts Guild. The Guild's mission is to enhance children's development by helping them to explore their authenticity through creativity education. Alex is deeply committed to helping others live more authentically and knows firsthand that it's important to start this journey when we are children.

Alex was born in the Soviet Union but at the age of thirteen moved to New York City. Alex shared with me that when living in the Soviet Union, he felt like an outsider because of his dark skin and being Jewish, and then when living in the United States, he felt like an outsider because he was an immigrant and did not know English when he first arrived in the country. Growing up in a very controlled environment, Alex felt lost—he felt disconnected and unaware of who he was.

His turning point came in his mid-twenties when he participated in a weekend retreat with an international men's group whose mission is to support men's growth, health, and success. Alex has continued to participate in men's groups since that life-changing moment. He told me: "As men, we feel pressure to hide our emotions and get messages like 'men don't cry.' If the way in which we want to behave doesn't accord with the image that society has of men, we'll try to push that down... Through this work, I've learned how to get out of my own way so that I can be more authentic."

Alex finally feels comfortable in his own skin and like he can show up in the world without hiding aspects of himself. But he also notes, and rightly so: "Authenticity is about choosing when to be authentic, and it's a choice that's based on what's right in the situation. Sometimes I will adapt my behavior because it makes sense to do that... For example, authenticity isn't about being 100 percent uncensored all the time."

Alex's sentiment is one that I heard often during my interviews—the idea that while we work to be our Authentic Self, there are times when we need to modify how we behave for personal, familial, societal, and organizational reasons. People told me that while there are moments when they choose to not behave entirely as their Authentic Self because it doesn't make sense to, they struggle with how to cast this intentional act of modifying their behavior. If they change their behavior and act in a way they want to, how can it be that they're not being true to themselves?

This is where the concept of the Adapted Self comes in, which introduces a new way of looking at the practice of living and leading authentically. The Adapted Self is an essential part of personal identity and a critical element of the authenticity journey. Some of us spend much time living as our Adapted Self because it feels far more fulfilling than it does to conform or mask to fit in, and it feels more practical than the Authentic Self in a given moment.

Your Adapted Self

Description	Key Attributes	How It Feels
Who you are when you willingly choose to alter your behavior from how your Authentic Self would act, to meet your needs and others' needs	• You feel like you have the *choice* to alter your behavior from how your Authentic Self would behave, and you do so willingly • Still a reflection of your values, beliefs, needs, desires, thoughts, emotions, and traits • You feel belonging in your interactions with others	• Empowering • Like alignment • Satisfying • Strategic

The Adapted Self observes that sometimes your needs and the needs of others will require you to behave outside the strict definition of who you truly are, and you feel comfortable in exercising the choice to do this. As your Adapted Self, you're aware of the options you have in how to act along the Seven Behavioral Dimensions and you make decisions to adapt your behavior given the demands and circumstances of the situation—you self-regulate.

For example, this is the self that wants to be direct in telling a loved one what we think or feel, but because we know that our directness may hurt them, we choose to tone down our message. It's the self that wants to stay quiet in team meetings because of nervousness, but we know it's better for our profile-building to speak and so we choose to do that instead. Or it's our pessimistic self (part of our bad or ugly Authentic Self) that always wants to point out that the glass is half empty, but we often choose to self-censor because we want our loved ones to confide in us. (And while I'm mentioning the bad/ugly side to who we really are, many of us already regularly adapt our behavior to be less dark because it serves us and others. As Drew Dudley told me during our teapot chat, "If your Authentic Self is mean and cynical, then don't be f*cking authentic, because it'll be bad for you and others.")

Here are other examples of the Adapted Self:

- You may hold back in sharing your dissenting viewpoint at a dinner party. It serves your needs—it would take a while to explain your thoughts and you can't sermonize for thirty minutes at the dinner table; or you slept for only five hours the night before and are too tired to share; or you're just shy. And it serves others' needs—these are your spouse's colleagues and your spouse will be pissed if you rock the boat. So you eat another piece of pie instead.

- As a mother of young children, you may be staying in a job that you like but don't love. It serves some of your needs—you are being paid decently to work at a reputable organization and you're utilizing your skills. Yes, the job may not meet some of your needs—especially your desire for a more senior role with a better title, more responsibility, and higher pay. But you note that your decision to stay in your current role serves others' needs—your hours are more flexible than they would be in a senior role, which means that you're better able to juggle your career with raising your children. So you stay put until your little ones get a bit older.

These examples highlight four aspects of the Adapted Self:

1   You've evaluated your needs and the needs of others in the situation.

2 You feel like you have the *choice* to alter your behavior from your Authentic Self in any of the Seven Behavioral Dimensions to meet those needs.

3 You exercise your choice willingly.

4 You feel aligned and empowered, which is very different from how you feel when you're performing.

The Adapted Self may be a minor tweak of your Authentic Self or it may involve significant behavioral change, but, in self-regulating, you feel comfortable exercising your choice to alter your behavior along any of the Seven Behavioral Dimensions. Even if you would have preferred to be your Authentic Self in this moment and it doesn't feel like a full expression of your authenticity, in choosing to alter your behavior you still feel aligned with your thoughts, feelings, and behaviors. This is why, when you show up as your Adapted Self, you're still in the zone of empowerment. As your Adapted Self, you'll never feel disempowered.

In *Quiet*, her best-selling book on the power of introversion, Susan Cain outlines Free Trait Theory, which essentially says that we are born with certain personality traits (like introversion), but we act out of character when it is in the service of "core personal projects." Cain notes, "[I]ntroverts are capable of acting like extroverts for the sake of work they consider important, people they love, or anything they value highly." Poignantly, she also explores the impact of this adaptive behavior on authenticity: "Yes, we are only pretending to be extroverts, and yes, such inauthenticity can be morally ambiguous (not to mention exhausting), but if it's in the service of love or a professional calling, then we're doing just as Shakespeare advised [To thine own self be true]." [1]

An essential question to explore when thinking about what your Adapted Self looks like is, "How much altering of behavior feels right to me?" If you are altering your behavior to the point that you're feeling unhappy because you're doing it against your desires (you don't feel like you have a choice *but* to change your behavior in order to get ahead) or you're feeling disempowered because you're not being even an iota of who you are, you're now into the land of performing. So your ultimate goal in leveraging the Three Selves continuum is to flow between your Authentic Self and Adapted Self—the zone of empowerment—as much as possible.

Flow between Being Authentic and Adaptive

One of the questions I hear most often with regard to being authentic is, "When does it make sense to be my Authentic Self versus my Adapted Self?" Or put another way, "When do I need to choose to alter my behavior from my authentic way of being to instead show up in an adapted way?"

This is a critical reflection point for many of us. We'll each have a different answer based on who our Authentic Self is, which behavioral dimensions are important to us and which ones we are less fussed about, what our needs are, what the needs of those around us are, and what adapting looks like and means for us.

Many of the people I interviewed shared their views on changing their behavior to get ahead in the workplace (which is where, I suspect, this question likely also plagues a number of you), and, not surprisingly, offered the following: When we're pushed to conform and mask throughout the workday, day after day, we ought to quit, because constantly having to show up as our Performing Self will suck us dry. But when it comes to flowing between our Authentic Self and Adapted Self, people recognized that this experience is less clear-cut and far more nuanced than to say, "always be 100 percent authentic," or "challenge the culture," or "don't do it," or "leave."

Heidi Levine, a leader at a global law firm, told me that at the age of thirty-four she joined the executive committee at her firm. Before starting, she was told by older and more experienced members that she should "just listen and not speak" at the meetings. As this didn't sit well with her, Heidi started speaking as soon as she joined. She was quickly pulled aside by a male firm leader, who told her not to speak unless she vetted her thoughts through him first.

Heidi shared with me that her immediate reaction was to buck what was asked of her. But she paused to reflect on how to be strategic about what to do. She wanted to be true to her authentic spirit, but she also recognized that being uncensored wouldn't help her as the new and youngest kid on the block: "I decided to keep speaking. I did temper a bit in what I said though, but I wasn't conforming. I was more strategic in when I spoke and what I said in order to have my voice be heard and to have a bigger impact. I also learned that I could still be authentic by listening and not speaking in a meeting, but then sharing afterward. The point is to be strategic in *how* you will be successful."

I also asked Joyce Roche, the former *Fortune* 500 company executive I talked about in chapter 8, about how she landed on how much altering of her behavior felt right over the course of her career. In noting that this isn't always an easy experience, Joyce shared an excellent insight:

It's important to go through phases. First, understand the environment you find yourself in. Then ask yourself, "What is acceptable? What is rewarded here?" and you do this by observing leaders and their behaviors. The next phase is to ask yourself, "What expectations work for me and what don't?" If most of the expectations work, then you'll adapt here and there—for example, in how you present and speak. Maybe you'll say, "I won't go the full extreme of the expectations, but I'll be somewhere in the middle." But maybe you'll say that the dial has moved too far and "if this is what is expected, this is not the right place for me." So the imbalance comes when you feel at your core that you're compromising your value system and integrity. When it feels like there's too much modification required, then you should stop adapting and get out. If it feels acceptable for you to adapt, then do it.

This is great advice. In her words of wisdom, Joyce is emphasizing the power of choice and suggesting that you be thoughtful and strategic about how you want to adapt your behavior; check in to see what feels right; and know when to stop modifying your behavior when you're into the zone of performing and, therefore, compromising your values.

To build on what Joyce and others shared with me about flowing between being authentic and adaptive, I can't emphasize enough how crucial it is that you have a strong understanding of your preferences along the Seven Behavioral Dimensions. By doing a deep dive into your preferences, you'll better understand how you would act in each of the dimensions if there were no negative consequences for your behaviors (i.e., if you were to be your Authentic Self); in which behavioral dimensions you're willing to adapt your behavior and in what circumstances; what the behavioral adjustments would look like; and what your limits are for adapting your behaviors.

In addition to doing a deep dive into the Seven Behavioral Dimensions, the other crucial practice to leverage in determining when to be authentic and when to adapt is what I call the "Be Authentic or Adaptive Reflection" (BAAR), which requires that you reflect on and respond to the following two key questions:

1   What are my "must do" or "must be" authentic behaviors along the Seven Behavioral Dimensions? (These are behaviors that are non-negotiable for you. You *must* be your Authentic Self by showing up in these ways along these dimensions.)

2   What are the behavioral dimensions in which I'm comfortable adapting, and what does my adaptive behavior look like in these dimensions? (In these dimensions, and in these ways, you're good to behave as your Adapted Self.)

The BAAR will assist you with the intense level of self-reflection and strategic thinking that will be required to be more adaptive or authentic going forward. Your answers to these questions will create the foundation you need in order to live as authentically as possible and be adaptive where it serves you. Your answers will help you to live in alignment, and move away from experiencing the negative feelings that come from performing, including feeling like you're "selling out."

I'll paint the picture for you by turning the BAAR mirror on myself. In showing you how I decide whether to be authentic or adapt along the behavioral dimensions, I'll demonstrate how you can leverage this methodology to help you remain anchored in the zone of empowerment.

BAAR QUESTION #1
My "must do" or "must be" authentic behaviors:
It's very important to me that I choose to express my emotions freely, both verbally and non-verbally. For example, I want to laugh loudly, cry openly, and use lots of hand and body gestures and facial expressions (and if you've ever seen me speak to a group, this all screams!). This is a "must do" area for me. Performing here feels excruciating for me.

It's also very important to me that I be authentic in the words I use when speaking. In most moments, I don't give a shit about saying whatever the hell I want (ha)! I flow between using fancy words, street slang, and a potty-mouth, regardless of the audience.

Another "must do" behavior along the Seven Behavioral Dimensions ties back to appearance. It's very important to me to be as authentic as possible in how I dress. I view my body as a canvas and an expression of who I am. I want to be able to wear bright colors and patterns, edgy styles, and funky jewelry, and rock piercings and tattoos. If I wear clothing with graphics or wording, they have to be in alignment with my values. I'll adapt how I dress to a certain extent (I won't wear clubbing clothes to a business meeting, for instance), but I deliberately challenge corporate conservatism when it comes to appearance. And, in my view, my appearance ought to be the least menacing of the behavioral dimensions when it comes to my career advancement. Performing here feels really disempowering to me.

BAAR QUESTION #2
THE DIMENSIONS in which I'm comfortable adapting and how:
I'm comfortable adapting how I speak. I think it makes sense for me as a public speaker, in particular, to play with my voice, pace, intonation, and pitch. For example, I know that when I drop my pitch in male-dominated audiences I seemingly sound more "powerful" and "authoritative." When I do this, do I actually become more powerful and authoritative? No, but I'm good to (sometimes) make this behavioral adjustment, especially if it will help shield against biases. I flow between being authentic and adaptive in the content I share and how I act in different circumstances. The extent to which I will share my thoughts, opinions, cultural differences, dissenting views, and experiences; say yes, no, or maybe; and draw boundaries, all depends on the environment I'm in, whose company I am in, how much of a container has been created for me to share safely, and, frankly, how I'm

feeling. (For example, I will self-censor my opinions less when I'm tired or stressed; the brain has decreased ability to exercise willpower in these states.).

Because I want to feel aligned as much as possible, I use the BAAR to help me stay anchored in the zone of empowerment by being as authentic and/or adaptive as possible. Authenticity is a journey and I'm on it, so on some days I feel more courageous to be authentic, while on others I'm good to adapt. What I can tell you is that the BAAR is an imperative reflection tool you can use in your efforts to live and lead more in alignment with the Authenticity Principle.

IN THE coming chapter, we'll dig into how you can practice being authentic and adaptive by looking at a range of practical strategies to implement in the way you live.

9

Practice Being Authentic and Adaptive

*And the day came when the risk to remain tight in a bud
was more painful than the risk it took to blossom.*

ANAÏS NIN[1]

"JUST BE yourself."

How many times have you been given that advice in the context of meeting someone new, doing an interview, starting a new job, going on a first date, or hanging out with new friends? It's great advice, but how do you actually make it happen?

To live authentically, it's not enough to know who you are and embrace it, you need to *take action* by engaging in behavior that enables you to bring your Authentic Self to life. It's all about leveraging techniques and exercises that will help you push away from your Performing Self in order to show up at the very least as your Adapted Self and preferably as your Authentic Self, in as many of the Seven Behavioral Dimensions as possible with yourself and others.

But choosing to be authentic can be hard when facing the pressure to conform, the fear of judgments, and other possible negative consequences. I talked to Lori Simpson, an executive leadership coach who has expertise in neurocoaching, about concepts put forth in the book *Immunity to Change: How to*

Overcome It and Unlock the Potential in Yourself and Your Organization by Robert Kegan and Lisa Laskow Lahey. In their work, Kegan and Lahey highlight that resistance to change is largely the result of hidden mindsets designed to protect us from disappointment or fear.

In discussing their work, Lori emphasized that in order to behave differently, "first you have to make a choice to do something or become something. This is an essential piece, but it's not enough. You then need to *act* on the choice. And this is hard work for most of us. Even though we want to change, very few of us actually do. Oftentimes, we have competing belief systems or our belief systems are unconscious—they run below our level of awareness, and we don't even realize what we're choosing. And unless we uncover these hidden belief systems, they can keep us stuck in a current pattern of thinking and being (acting)."

In breaking this down further for me, Lori explained:

> Decisions and action require emotion. In order to go through the pain and discomfort of change (yes, our brains actually activate in pain centers when we make change), we need to have a vision of the future that's so compelling that it evokes sufficient emotion to move us to take action in the present. Once we have a compelling vision, we can begin to identify what needs to be true about our thoughts and behaviors in the present to bring us closer to the future we desire. In the context of authenticity, it's about identifying what we need to believe, think, and do to bring ourselves closer to being our authentic selves.

As Lori's comments suggest, living in accordance with the Authenticity Principle is a process of change. It requires that you surround yourself with support, listen to your body, and start by taking small actions to change your thoughts and actions.

Recall: Authenticity is a practice, in that you develop your abilities to be authentic the more you commit, try, and persevere in doing this. It's like exercising to build new muscle mass in the body—your ability to be authentic will strengthen the more you partake in actions to learn about who you are, exercise the choice to live out who you are, and push yourself to be your Authentic Self despite your fears and discomfort. Put another way, the more you exercise your "authenticity muscle," the more developed it will become, and being authentic will eventually become your default behavior.

In this chapter, we'll explore how to practice being authentic and adaptive, starting with how to build your authenticity muscle.

Be Deliberate with Your Authenticity Practice

In Carol Dweck's leading work on mindsets, she asserts that individuals who hold a growth mindset about their abilities—those who believe that hard work, dedication, learning, and resilience can help them to grow and develop—will be more successful.[2] I have seen this as well in my work in the authenticity space: the same spirit emanates from people who live by the Authenticity Principle. Those who believe that they can make choices, work hard, and learn skills to be increasingly authentic are more likely to *practice* being themselves.

In psychology, the "Conscious Competence Ladder" is a model that sets out four stages of learning, and our related thoughts and emotions, when we are acquiring new skills. According to the model, as we build competence in a new skill, we move through four stages:

1 Unconsciously incompetent: we don't know that we don't have the skill or that we need to develop it.
2 Consciously incompetent: we know that we don't have the skill, but we want to develop it.

3 Consciously competent: we have the skill, but it requires concentrated effort to use the skill.

4 Unconsciously competent: we have heightened ability in the skill and we seamlessly use it.[3]

In developing your authenticity muscle, the goal is to achieve unconscious competence, where being authentic is simply your way of being. But to get there, you have to work through the other stages.

Learning from neuroscience is reassuring: it tells us that practicing any behavior or thought regularly and frequently brings about change. Therefore, continually practicing authenticity will make it easier to be yourself. What we currently know from neuroscience is this:[4]

- The brain is plastic, meaning that it can be changed (neuroplasticity).

- When we change our mental activity—and more specifically, our thoughts/thinking—we create new neural pathways in the brain that lead to new ways of behaving (neurons that fire together, wire together).

- Every day, the brain generates new stem cells, some of which will go to where they're needed for learning, and over a few months they will connect with other cells to create new neural circuitry. We can direct the cells to places of new learning—and, therefore, new ways of behaving—through our mental activity and our thoughts (neurogenesis).

Dr. Rick Hanson notes in his book *Buddha's Brain*, "[Experience] makes enduring changes in the physical tissues of your brain which affect your well-being, functioning, and relationships."[5] In other words, in addition to your thoughts, the experiences you have really do matter for rewiring your brain, and so changing your behavior (and even thinking about or pic- turing how you're going to change it) is critical to changing your mindset and to becoming unconsciously competent. So, inten- tionally and frequently practicing authenticity will actually rewire your brain, making it easier for you to be who you are and for your actions to be aligned with your true self.

Here are a few key strategies you can leverage in building your authenticity muscle:

Have a Plan
Plan in advance how you want to be more authentic going forward with yourself and with others, using the following techniques:

- **The power of self-coaching:** This is the practice of pre-select- ing words of encouragement, affirmation, and guidance you can tell yourself when The Voice is saying you ought to per- form. (For example, I tell myself things like "Just do it," "Just say it," "Just be it," etc.—watch for my rack of lamb example coming up.) The great thing about self-coaching is that you don't need anyone else to do it, you can do it anywhere, and it's easy to get good at it if you keep doing it.

- **The power of scripting:** Here I'm talking about actually plan- ning out what you will say to others in a situation, by either writing down the script or rehearsing in your head what you'll say (ideally, you'll do both). Essentially, this plants language into your unconscious brain for future retrieval.

- **The power of visualization:** Recall that Lori Simpson, the executive leadership coach with expertise in neurocoaching, discussed the importance of having a vision in my conver- sation with her. I also alluded to visualization above when I noted the importance of experiences for rewiring your brain. With visualization, you want to plan out how you'll behave differently in future situations and repeatedly picture yourself doing this. Like scripting, you're tucking future behavior into your unconscious brain, and you're engaging in an emotional response to an experience even before you actually have it, which builds a commitment to the change and the capacity to follow through.

Leverage Previous Authentic Experiences

Reflect on the experience of being authentic after you've behaved in such a way, either with yourself or with others, so that you're able to replicate the experience again by leveraging the following techniques:

- **The power of reflection:** After an experience of practicing authenticity, when you were true to yourself or in an interaction with someone else, reflect on how it felt for you, explore what behavior resonated and what didn't, and consider how you will change your behavior going forward. Then script and visualize the change you've decided to make.

- **The power of reward/recognition:** This is fun—consider rewarding yourself for being authentic in moments with yourself and with others. I'm not talking about cracking open the Dom or scarfing down three red velvet cupcakes. I'm mostly referring to giving yourself positive reinforcement, particularly through words of affirmation (for example, telling yourself, "See, I knew you could do it!" or "You've got this," or whatever language resonates with you) and repeating this language to inspire you to keep working at being more authentic. But this could also mean a mini-celebration—celebrating with yourself by doing something nice for yourself (for me, this would be a spa trip) or creating a symbol of the experience (for example, putting up a quote on the wall that will remind you of your courage, or buying a bracelet that you can wear as a reminder). A window into my life: I got a tattoo of the Sikh symbol for *Ik Onkar* (One Creator) on my left wrist a few years ago in order to encourage and celebrate my authenticity.

• **The power of positivity:** Start to track your moments of authenticity, both those you have with yourself and with others. For each experience, spend at least five minutes contemplating and, preferably, writing down the following:

  • When did this positive experience of authenticity happen?
  • Was it with yourself or with others?
  • In which environment did it take place?
  • How was the container created for you to be more of yourself?
  • How did you behave authentically?
  • Most importantly, how did you *feel* when you were being authentic? What positive feelings or sensations did you have in your body when you behaved like X?

Focus on the body sensations and feelings during your reflection and start to clock them going forward as markers for being authentic. Also, before you enter into a situation where you want to behave more authentically, think back to these positive memories of being yourself and reflect on the positive sensations and feelings you experienced when you were being authentic (you may even want to throw in some of the words of affirmation that you used earlier), as a way to prime yourself to be yourself.

Experiment with Being Yourself

In learning to practice being more authentic, you'll benefit from playing with the experience of being yourself. Experimenting with which behaviors and situations feel right for you to share—and which don't—is very important.

In my discussion with Jim Leipold, an executive director of a North American non-profit association, he emphasized the importance of finding opportunities that serve as "test kitchens for being authentic." Jim shared with me that, when coming out as a gay man, "I was looking for places where I could first go to test my newly articulated identity and seek social acceptance."

He looked for people with whom he felt safe exploring who he is and what barriers were causing him to perform. He knew these people would provide him with support and belonging because they accepted him for all of who he is, including his differences: "It's about testing how authenticity feels by experimenting and then being able to say, 'That felt good and this didn't.' And getting positive reinforcement from others along the way really helped." (Recall: as humans, we're a tribal species and so being relational matters.)

Others shared that experimenting with being yourself means taking risks. Savaria Harris, a senior lawyer in the pharmaceutical industry, had this to say: "It's important to build your muscle in a safe space; practice being authentic in safe spaces and then parlay this to other areas . . . It's a tall order to become authentic automatically, so pick areas of your life that are safe—like with friends or about personal boundaries—to practice in. This will give you the language for other areas that are harder to start in, like your professional life, because you may not have the right environment, or boss, etc."

This idea ties back into the concept of the green–yellow–red light self-assessment (which I first mentioned in chapter 1), that Tim Thompson, a chief operating officer of a division of a global bank, shared with me. When you are in the company of others and you choose the "red light," opting not to share a piece of yourself, it may expose an area that you didn't realize you view as being "off limits" to share or it may reveal that a safe environment for being authentic hasn't been created. You may fear being judged by the people you're with or feel shame about an aspect of who you are. When you choose the "yellow light," you may be tentatively dipping your big toe into the waters of living more authentically and this, too, is revealing. When you choose the "green light," this is a sweet spot for you—it's an authentic moment in the presence of others.

Consider ways in which you can begin sharing more "green light" aspects of yourself, starting immediately. Envisage the following: as you're getting ready to meet with friends or colleagues, picture yourself sharing an authentic side of yourself (e.g., sharing something you've been wanting to say or something about yourself you've not shared yet). Give thought to what you'd say/do and how/when. Then do it.

Authentic Living Insight
How to Be More Authentic When Sharing

In your commitment to live, work, and lead more authentically, you may feel vulnerable when having to choose when to share instead of staying silent, and what to say if you do choose to speak. As a first step, it can be helpful to tune in to how you've been behaving to date and determine if you've been sharing socially acceptable content rather than speaking your truth.

A key moment when many of us perform is during small talk, whether during social events, out running errands, networking, or around the watercooler. Consider how you've been performing when you respond to the following types of questions, and how you can share more authentically going forward:

———

Question: "How are you?"

Socially acceptable answer: "Great!" even if you actually want to quit the world and live in a forest

Authentic living insight: Give thought to replacing commonly used words like "great," "good," "fine," "busy" (can we all please agree never to use that word again?) with words that tie back to an experience you've just had and the emotions you're feeling. Example: "I'm better this week—last week was tough because of xyz, but I'm catching my breath this week."

Question: "How are the kids?"

Socially acceptable answer: "Oh, they're so great" even if you actually want to take them back to where they came from

Authentic living insight: Tell (more of) the truth by sharing a quick story about your kids or a challenge you're having with them.

Question: "How's work?"

Socially acceptable answer: "Busy, but great!" even if you hate what you do, are exhausted from the workload, and want to run screaming from the building most days

Authentic living insight: Share something you're working on that you're enjoying, or describe a challenge you're having.

Question: "What's new and exciting for you?"

Socially acceptable answer: Argh, this is probably one of the worst small-talk questions ever! Even when there is nothing "new and exciting" in your life, you'll probably feel pressure to come up with something "new and exciting" to say, so you take something that is actually low-to-medium-exciting and turn it into something medium-to-high-exciting.

Authentic living insight: Tell the truth ("I don't think anything new and exciting is going on . . .") and instead share what you want to

("What I can share is . . ."). Then ask the person a specific, personal question that will give rise to a more meaningful discussion. For example, "How is your health? Last time I saw you, you said you were having back pain," or "How is work these days? Last time I saw you, you said you were struggling with your workload. Is it getting better?" or even simply "What's filling your days as of late?"

Start Small, Then Go Big in Being Authentic

I was at a nice restaurant a while back and really wanted to eat the rack of lamb I had ordered with my fingers—I mean, grab the meat by the bone and gnaw down on it. I had a moment of "That's not how you're supposed to behave in a nice restaurant," but then I remembered the Authenticity Principle—I actually even said to myself, "Be yourself" (self-coaching!). So I did it. I know it doesn't sound like a big deal, but it was one small moment that's part of my larger commitment to being true to myself. (And how about this: the moment I did it, my friend said, "Oh, I wanted to do that too, but wasn't sure I should!" and then he picked up a rack from his plate and took a big bite.)

During my interviews for this book, several people spoke of the importance of starting off small with practicing authenticity—and I'm with them. There's no need or benefit to wildly unleashing your Authentic Self all at once to the world. It may be really hard for you to do it, and it may be downright off-putting to those around you if they haven't seen much of it before.

A key lesson about behavioral change is that it's all about small changes (and this is how the brain is rewired—by making repeated micro tweaks to behavior that, cumulatively, have a larger macro impact). In speaking with arts community leader and activist Seema Jethalal, she discussed the concept of "relentless incrementalism" in the context of taking action to engage in change. Seema noted that "it's about starting small with the *actions* one wants to take in order to create authentic change that is aligned with one's values."

In her book, *Presence: Bringing Your Boldest Self to Your Biggest Challenges*, Amy Cuddy describes these small behavioral changes as "self-nudging." She explains that self-nudges are minimal modifications to your behavior, which are intended to produce small psychological and behavioral improvements in the moment (for example, sitting more upright or placing your hands on your hips when speaking—behavior that will lead you to feel more confident). They are tiny tweaks with the potential to lead to big changes over time. Cuddy explains that self-nudges are very powerful because they're small and require minimal psychological and physical commitment, and the real magic is that while we think our attitudes will change our behavior, the reverse is true as well—attitudes follow from behaviors. So change your behavior, and it will ultimately change your thoughts and mindset.[6]

How do you determine what small nudges or changes to make? Strategically choose the behavioral dimensions in which you want to start being more authentic, even in small ways, and go for the low-hanging fruit first—the environments in which it feels easier to make these changes and situations that have low stakes. Not surprisingly, these "low risk" areas will be different for each of us. For some, the workplace is too sensitive a place to suddenly show up all uncensored and fist-pumping, so perhaps the starting point will be to practice at home with your family and at dinner parties with your friends.

Authentic Voices
Small Stakes Lead to Big Stakes

In our interview, Jai-Jagdeesh, a formidable musician and yogi, beautifully described how the process of practicing authenticity in "small stakes" situations has helped her to then do this in "big stakes" situations, and how good that feels. Here's how she explained it:

> I use "small stakes" situations to practice being me so that I can flip the switch to do it in bigger situations. A small stake for me would be when I'm invited to a family or friend thing and I tune in to myself and say, "Do I want to do this? Does this fill me with joy or anticipation? And if I don't do it, will I be okay with the aftermath?" It's about answering in a truthful way and then living the truth. Saying no to family and friends on these types of things is a good small step to learning how to be yourself in big stakes moments where it's harder to be authentic—like having a tough conversation with a team member or drawing a boundary by saying no to a loved one on something that's hard for them.

After years of conforming and masking in many areas of her life, one of my Black girlfriends decided to start being more of herself across the board, which for her meant discovering and revealing more of herself as a Black woman. She leveraged small stakes to help her build up to big stakes. She started by going to more Black community events and then moved on to big stakes like Black advocacy and empowerment circles, such as Black Lives Matter events. She also decided to wear her hair naturally, first on weekends among friends (small stakes, although this was a big thing for her too), then one courageous day in the workplace (bigger stakes), and I think now she might be gunning for a full-on Afro. And here's what these incremental steps have brought her: She's found her voice. At work, she feels more comfortable to share her dissent in meetings with leaders (despite her initial fears of being judged as the "difficult Black woman") and she openly shares with others that she is involved with Black Lives Matter and other cultural aspects of her life. She started small and was then able to go big with living more authentically.

You can do this too.

Surround Yourself with Authentic People

Authenticity is contagious. To be yourself as much as possible, it helps to surround yourself with others who model authentic behavior. Not only will you learn more about how to do it, you'll feel more comfortable being yourself around these inspiring people who will also help to hold you accountable. Observing others model and be their authentic selves in our presence helps to equip us with the tools to practice authenticity, and it also invites us to follow suit by being ourselves—a key component of the Authenticity Principle.

Authenticity is also contagious because when someone openheartedly shares their thoughts, emotions, vulnerabilities, and imperfections with you, it helps to create the intimacy and trust that is needed for you to share as well. The person is signaling that they're open to having you reciprocate by sharing, and that a safe space—or to borrow from yoga, as mentioned previously, the container—is being created for you to be your Authentic Self in that moment.

I've certainly had this experience. From observing Verna Myers and Annahid Dashtgard, both incredibly talented leadership and inclusion professionals, I've learned the beauty and strength of sharing my vulnerabilities in my interactions. From observing Stuart Knight, a global leadership speaker and author, I've learned that despite the negative consequences (for example, losing money by "firing" a client who pushes you to be someone you're not), choosing to be myself is worth it. And from observing Dr. Eddie Moore Jr., an activist and educator, I've learned that living your truth in as many of the behavioral dimensions as possible will actually feel like it's freeing you.

Since I started writing this book, never have I been more focused on living in the spirit of the Authenticity Principle. For example, I've been sharing openly with my family, friends, clients, team members, and even strangers about how hard it is to write a book (OMG, it is *not* easy!). I've been awash with feelings of insecurity, the impostor syndrome, failure, and more. But here's what's been fascinating: In these moments of great vulnerability for me, not only are people kind and empathetic, they open up and they share. I've heard a vast range of stories from people about the things that cause them to feel fear, such as entering a new relationship or leaving their current one, becoming parents, doing a good job of parenting, starting school or a new business, being promoted, and leading new team members. Because I opened up, they did.

Lastly, it's important to surround yourself with a *diverse range* of authentic people. If you surround yourself with people who look, sound, act, and are the same as you (that is, similar in personality, culture, gender, age, experience, profession, interests, and more), you'll most likely get the same type of modeling/ coaching/guidance on how to be authentic. So shake it up by surrounding yourself with a broad, diverse range of people from whom you can learn and be inspired, and by whom you can be held accountable.

Use Your Body as a Guidepost

Throughout this book, I've highlighted a mix of body and emotional awareness, self-reflection, and neuroscience-based strategies and practices to help you learn to live, work, and lead more authentically. I've been encouraging you to use the feelings and sensations in your body as a guidepost for when and how to practice being authentic. Specifically, when you increasingly find that being authentic *feels* amazing, you'll be more inclined to choose to do it.

The starting point is engaging in present awareness of how you're feeling and what you're sensing in your body. It's like taking a snapshot of your emotions and body sensations in a given moment so that you can measure to what extent you felt good about your behavior in that moment, notice the environment you were in, pay attention to the people you were with, and so on. It's about getting to the point where you can use your body to identify the amazing feelings that are connected to being yourself (whatever that feels like for you—for example, like flying, warm flutters through the heart and chest area, a joyous buzz throughout the body), and the oppressive sensations that are connected with performing (for example, nausea, heaviness in the chest, tingling at the back of the neck, muscle tightness, sweatiness, irritated digestive system).

So what are some strategies to help you use your body as a guidepost? Not surprisingly, the principal answers to this question tie back to mindfulness, like the yogis first suggested over six thousand years ago.

I define "mindfulness" as the process of gaining present awareness of what we're feeling and thinking, and being nonjudgmental about our observations. (It's not necessarily about lululemon pants, candles, incense, sitar music, and the half-lotus position.) As a mindfulness practitioner and teacher, I have embedded a number of mindfulness strategies throughout this book (some clearly labeled as such and others that are less evident—done by design because some people are automatically turned off when they hear the term "mindfulness"). In the remainder of this chapter, I'll be more explicit about how to leverage mindfulness and I'll highlight some of the great recommendations that life coach and yoga teacher Brigid Dineen shared with me.

In our discussion about using the body as a compass for helping us to be more authentic, Brigid noted that oftentimes you won't even know that you're performing or that your body is screaming, "Please be yourself!" This happens because when you're performing, you'll have a physical stress response in your body—your muscles will tense up, your breath will become shallow, your cortisol levels will go up, and you may self-soothe in unhealthy ways (drinking, over-eating, not sleeping, etc.). In these moments, your body is controlled by your sympathetic nervous system (SNS); your body is stuck in fight-or-flight mode and you may not even know it. In this state, you will, in fact, have a harder time accessing clear thoughts because your body is focusing on warding off threats and your mind is likely in managed freak-out mode—certainly not targeting beautiful, harmonious self-reflection. To gather what you're feeling and thinking, you'll need to consciously tune in.

The good news is that your body and mind are reflections of each other. You can use the body to calm the mind, which we now know is much more accessible than using the mind to calm the body. Tuning in to your bodily sensations in a given situation, and then leading or directing your thoughts and emotions with physical techniques and practices, will help you to immediately focus when you're trying to figure out how to behave, what you're feeling, and what's getting in the way of you behaving more authentically.

There are a few easily accessible, simple ways to make this happen, and I'll take you through them now. But before I do, please note that I put all of these strategies under the category of mindfulness because they either bring you into current awareness of what you're feeling and thinking, or they'll help to shift your state for the better. They're a gift, so use them!

Engage in Diaphragm Breathing

If you ask me (and so many other experts), this is the number one thing you can do physically in order to change your life (to be authentic, calm, confident, joyous, centered, effective—the list of positives goes on and on). It's my magic bullet. Breathing deeply can immediately help to undo many of the body's stress responses because it helps to pull us out of the fight-or-flight state ruled by the SNS, and into the calmer, more contemplative and contented state governed by the parasympathetic nervous system (PNS). Simply breathing deeply and slowly into your belly will help you to access what you are physically sensing, feeling, and even thinking—awareness that is lost to you when you're using the shallow breathing that comes with fight-or-flight mode.

By breathing deeply, what I mean is taking a slow, fulsome breath on your inhalation (ideally through your nose), which will cause your diaphragm to contract and move downward, enabling you to push your belly out and to fill your lungs with air right to the bottom. The inverse applies on your exhalation—you slowly pull your belly all the way in, causing your diaphragm to relax and pull upward, and the air right from the bottom of your lungs to be pushed up through your mid-chest to your upper chest then out.

Use Body Postures to Change How You're Feeling

In her research on the effectiveness of power poses, Amy Cuddy emphasizes that your body changes your mind, your mind changes your behavior, and your behavior changes outcomes. In both her book *Presence* and her TED Talk, Cuddy boldly declares, "How you carry your body shapes how you carry out your life." [7] For example, she explains how putting yourself into a power position (standing up straight, feet hip-distance apart, facing straight—in yoga, think *tadasana* or "mountain pose"—with your hands on your hips) will automatically help to decrease cortisol (the stress hormone) and increase testosterone (the confidence hormone), which will actually help you to feel more empowered to be yourself. To learn more about how to leverage power positions, I highly recommend watching Cuddy's TED Talk (a zillion others have!).

Practice Self-Care of Your Body and Mind

This is going to sound rather obvious, but self-care will help you to live more authentically. Self-care will help you to better track, and alter, how you're feeling and what you're thinking. So, sleep at least seven to eight hours, eat well, avoid sugar like the plague (think inflammation, which is linked to most diseases), drink truckloads of water, stay clear of alcohol and drugs, exercise, and engage in some form of restorative practice for the mind and body each day.

What do I mean by "restorative practice"? It could be meditation; *pranayama* or breathing exercises; yoga or stretching; a warm bath; a relaxing walk; creative pursuits, such as drawing, painting, dancing, or drumming; or snuggling with your beloved, be that a spouse, lover, cat, or dog. All of these calming activities will help you to better access what you're feeling and thinking, and will help you be more authentic.

Adopt Other Effective Mindfulness Strategies

In *Buddha's Brain*, Dr. Rick Hanson outlines a few techniques that are worth mentioning because they're effective and easy to use:

- **Touch your lips:** How much do I love this strategy?! Not just because I do it all the time and I had no idea of its benefits (again, your body knows what you need), but because you can do this absolutely anywhere, anytime, and no one will know why you're doing it. Essentially, PNS fibers are spread throughout your lips and so when you touch your lips, it causes you to relax. The human body is so amazing!

- **Picture your "happy place"**: Dr. Hanson outlines how using imagery activates the right hemisphere of the brain and quiets our internal noise (i.e., The Voice). You can use your own "happy place" imagery to help activate your PNS. (For me, this means picturing a deserted white-sand beach with crystal-clear blue-green water or the *parikarma* of the Harmandir Sahib in Amritsar, Punjab, which is the holiest place for the Sikhs.) What makes picturing your "happy place" imagery even more impactful is to daydream about its amazingness; use your five senses to give thought to what it's like to experience this place in person (what does it look, sound, smell, taste, and feel like?); and reflect on the positive feelings that you have about being there.[8]

The last strategy I'll recommend here is one of my all-time favorites, which is simply to smile. Smiling activates the release of neuropeptides (tiny molecules that allow neurons to communicate), which help to fight stress and to send messages to the body about how you're feeling. Smiling also causes the release of "happy" hormones, which not only help to relax your body but also act as an antidepressant and mood lifter. So smile—even if no one is watching!

Before moving on to the next chapter, let's pause to reflect on how we can practice being more authentic and adaptive going forward by leveraging the strategies discussed above.

Reflection Moment
- Think of a time when you've willingly made the choice to adapt your behavior from your Authentic Self
  - with family members
  - with friends

- in the work environment
- in social situations

Why did you adapt your behavior in these examples? How did you feel when you adapted your behavior?

- Using the "Be Authentic or Adaptive Reflection" (BAAR):
  - What are your "must do" or "must be" authentic behaviors along the Seven Behavioral Dimensions? *(See pages 23-24 for the detailed description of the dimensions.)*
  - What are the behavioral dimensions in which you're comfortable adapting, and what does your adaptive behavior look like in these dimensions?

- What are a few "small stake" changes you can make to your behavior to be more authentic and adaptive?

- Who are a few people who you can surround yourself with in order to be more authentic and adaptive?

- How will you use your body as a guidepost going forward to help you be more authentic and adaptive?

AS YOU explore these strategies and practices, it's key that you use what works for you in finding your own path to living, working, and leading more authentically. There is no "one size fits all." Everyone's path will be different based on their respective backgrounds, experiences, differences, cultures, values, needs, and more. What matters most is that you figure out who *you* are and what is getting in your way of being that person, and then take action to be authentic and adaptive in ways that work for you.

Now let's explore the power of authentic leadership.

10

Leaders, Be the Change

Leadership is a choice, not a position.
STEPHEN R. COVEY

RECALL THE image of the workplace as a sandbox, which I discussed in chapter 6—a place where there is a strong tidal wave of informal and formal pressure to conform and mask to get ahead (think of messages such as "Be more assertive," "Be more expressive," "Self-promote more directly"). Unfortunately, people who feel different—often women and those from diverse communities—are likeliest to feel this pressure. Meanwhile, organizations continue to struggle with poor morale, low engagement, and high attrition rates, particularly among these communities.

Authentic leadership offers a disruptive approach to shift how we're addressing these difficult workplace issues.

In the sandbox, the leaders—those who motivate, inspire, incentivize, and direct others to follow them—are responsible for developing their organization's culture by way of the formal and informal behavioral rules they create, enforce, and reward. How leaders think, what they say, and how they behave matters tremendously because some within the sandbox will automatically benefit from those ways, while others will get left behind.

As a leader, whether you're a parent, teacher, priest, politician, sports coach, or otherwise, you have the ability to influence others in decision-making, to welcome differences, and to bring out the best in every person in your organization. You can directly affect the success of your organization by creating an environment where others flourish based on who they are.

The change starts with you.

If you live, work, and lead in alignment with the Authenticity Principle, you'll foster a culture where everyone feels safe, comfortable, and valued for showing up as their true self. In this way you can bring out the best in every member of your organization (or family, classroom, congregation, constituency, sports team, and more).

Your Team Is Watching You

We know that when leaders "walk the talk" on their stated values—when they behave authentically—employees are more likely to develop trusting relationships with those leaders, enjoy working with them, experience higher levels of workplace well-being and meaning because of them, and are more likely to feel more engaged, satisfied, and empowered.[1] Authentic leaders don't just talk about the importance of authenticity; they take *actual steps* to cultivate environments and relationships that encourage trust, motivation, optimism, and inclusiveness.

On inclusiveness, research shows that it drives organizational financial performance (the actual bottom line) because leveraging differences in viewpoints, leadership styles, and more leads to greater creativity, increased innovation, improved decision-making, stronger customer orientation, and higher levels of employee satisfaction.[2] When people feel valued for what they bring to the table, they are more likely to contribute, collaborate, create, innovate, and feel better in the workplace. The ultimate goal is to create a culture where differences are valued and authenticity is normalized.

I've had the pleasure of working with Kelvin Tran, Senior Vice President and Chief Auditor for the TD Bank Group, through my inclusion work. Kelvin has an incredible life story. In getting to know each other, Kelvin told me about his cultural background—he is of Chinese descent but was born in Vietnam. He also shared about his experiences as a refugee coming to Canada as a child in 1979, a part of his life that he's only recently started to talk openly about. Kelvin's family fled Vietnam by boat—his parents woke their children up in the middle of the night to leave. "We were at sea for six days, packed like sardines on the boat—for six days I was in a fetal position and could barely go to the bathroom." Kelvin went on to share, "We ran out of food and the engine blew out, but we were saved by a navy ship and landed in a refugee camp in Indonesia. We were sponsored by my uncle in Montreal and we came to Canada when I was still in grade school."

Kelvin told me he used to not talk openly about his refugee status, feeling embarrassed by it. But as he's become more comfortable and confident about who he is as an individual, he feels like he can be more authentic in general but specifically at work, and now he readily brings up his story: "I have seen a shift in myself in what I now talk about. I think of my parents' courage and I feel very proud of my background. For example, when I'm speaking on a panel, I used to only talk about job stuff, but now I mention Vietnam and my refugee background—and I get much better feedback."

In helping others to be more authentic in the workplace, Kelvin advises, "If a leader says, 'Do X,' then first know and understand *why* you're being asked to do this behavior. If you believe in it, then act on it. If you are doing it for conformity's sake, then don't do it." When asked for his top tip on how to transform organizational culture, Kelvin said, "Leaders must go first." Those powerful words continue to resonate with me.

In our interview, pieces of which I shared earlier, New York University law professor Kenji Yoshino also talked about the importance of leaders going first to combat covering. He noted that if we want to create a work environment where team members can be more of themselves, leaders have to "uncover" first, which means revealing aspects of themselves to others in the workplace, including their cultural differences. As a result, people will trust these leaders more. This idea was echoed in the comments of Kristy Carscallen, a senior partner at the global professional services firm KPMG. "Trust causes people to open up," she told me in our interview. "They won't doubt your intentions."

Trust. This word came up repeatedly during my interviews as an essential ingredient for being impactful as a leader. "My success as a leader depends on whether people trust me," said Rob Granatstein, managing partner of the global law firm Blake, Cassels & Graydon LLP. "That trust comes by way of building a relationship painstakingly over days, weeks, and months. And people will only have that trust if they think and feel I'm being real in who I am and what I'm saying to them."

The "tone at the top" permeates an entire organization. As a leader, you must model the behavior that you would like everyone to embody. Through self-reflection and the practice of choosing authenticity on a consistent basis, you hone your ability to be yourself—and only then can you encourage authenticity throughout your organization. Consistency is key here. As Richard Meade, Vice President and Chief Legal Officer for Prudential's International Insurance businesses, told me, "When people can see that you're passionate about something; when you follow through and do the things you say you will do; when people around you believe that what they are seeing and hearing they can actually rely on; and when you do all this consistently, you create a sense of trust that helps build the culture of your team or organization."

Recognize and Address Your Privilege

As a leader you've got more status, power, and pull than your team members. And, of course, you'll be most likely to set organizational rules based on your own preferred behaviors, so it'll be easier for you to be authentic than it will be for others. There's tremendous privilege in this dynamic. Through your behaviors, you determine who feels included on your team and who doesn't. Because of this, it's incumbent upon you to take responsibility for the impact of your actions.

Remember, your team members are watching you to see how you behave and what you expect of others. If, through your actions, you push them to conform by behaving more like you and they don't want to do this, the cascading impact will be profound: unhappiness, disengagement, and retention issues. But if you encourage everyone to bring their whole, true self to work, you'll be better able to tap into their insights, skills, creativity, and differences. Recall that leveraging diversity of thought, background, and experience enhances decision-making, innovation, employee engagement, and financial performance.

Recognizing and addressing your privilege can feel downright uncomfortable, but the impact is even worse when you don't. I spoke about the accountability that comes with privilege in my conversation with Reva Seth, who is a best-selling author and the founder of The Optimal Living Lab. We discussed the fact that some of us have a heightened ability to practice authenticity more consistently than others *because of* our privilege, which we enjoy thanks to our status, age, financial stability, job security, and autonomy, in addition to other personal and cultural identity characteristics (like race/ethnoculture and gender identity). Reva aptly explained that when we are better positioned than others to practice authenticity (for instance, because of our authority), it's important that we be mindful of how our behavior impacts the people who report to us or who we indirectly impact.

If you don't recognize and address your privilege, it will have a detrimental impact on others, even unknowingly, and you won't be living, working, and leading in accordance with the Authenticity Principle. For example, if you're being authentic as an emotionally expressive extrovert, but you are pushing emotionally restrained introverted team members to be more like you and your version of authenticity, then your behavior is not in alignment with the spirit of the Authenticity Principle. In our interview, Dr. Catherine Zahn, President and CEO of the Centre for Addiction and Mental Health, a globally renowned hospital, confessed that many years ago she had been working with a direct report for three years before she realized that she was trying to turn that person into her. She could feel the adverse impact on her team member. Vowing never to do this again, Dr. Zahn works very hard at encouraging her team members to be themselves.

Now, there may be moments when you feel team members ought to alter their actions along the Seven Behavioral Dimensions in order to be more successful or to meet expectations. For example, you'd like a team member to be more direct and expressive during a team meeting or client pitch. In these cases, I suggest that you be transparent about why you want to see the behavioral adaptation, frame the behavioral adaptation positively (i.e., it's not because the team member is flawed), encourage this adaptation only for limited moments as required, and invite the person to choose whether they want to adapt or not.

It's essential to stress to your team members that adapting their behavior in specific circumstances does not, and should not, require permanent behavioral change. They should make a conscious decision to adapt their behavior only when they think it's appropriate, and you can help to coach them on when and why that may be the case.

It's much easier to choose to be adaptive in limited, required moments (i.e., be your Adapted Self) than it is to act like someone you're not all the time (i.e., be your Performing Self). If you keep pressuring team members to perform all the time or across all the dimensions, they will leave your organization. So when you encourage a team member to adapt, specifically target what you want to see and frame it in the positive. For example, you would tell your team member, "You're a very effective presenter—at our weekly team meetings, it may serve you to speak a bit louder so that everyone can hear you well, and to help you do that, you may want to consider sitting up straighter and leaning into the table a bit more." But what you don't want to do is vilify your team member's behavior or imply that something is wrong with their behavioral differences.

I asked talent management leader and leadership coach Michelle Grocholsky if there are areas in her work interactions where she expects team members to conform or change their behaviors. This was her revealing response: "It's a delicate dance. On one hand, I want to encourage my team to be their genuine, authentic selves; and on the other, it's important that they 'know their audience' and tailor their approach." What does Michelle do about this balancing act?

> Before entering into situations where they may feel compelled to conform, I encourage my team to first spend time reflecting on how they want to show up and what that looks like for them, and then to reflect on what they believe the audience's expectations and needs are. This will help them to identify how to bring out their genuine approach (for example, a sense of humor) while balancing what the needs of the group are (such as data-driven analysis). It helps to

spot instances where they may feel compelled to be someone other than themselves, and come up with tactics they can use to come back to how they want to show up.

Michelle's comments underscore how as a leader you can help your team members to flow between being authentic and adaptive, by encouraging them to practice self-reflection and to exercise choice.

Become an Authentic Leader

When you live more in alignment with the Authenticity Principle, you'll bring this spirit to your workplace, and you'll naturally encourage your team members to do the same, thereby helping to create a more empowered, engaged, inclusive, and innovative organization. You'll see how the domino effect of being authentic is extremely powerful, so you'll keep doing it. It's like sprinkling "authenticity dust" into the air at work—and seeing how it brings magic to the environment.

So, what specifically does an authentic leader do?

Authentic leaders are true to how they *want* to behave—they may show up as their Adapted Self, but they try their darndest to be their Authentic Self, and they abhor having to be their Performing Self. Even in the face of making themselves vulnerable, they consistently choose to show up as their Authentic Self and Adapted Self as much as possible.

Authentic leaders share the following characteristics:

- They are highly self-reflective.
- They are willing to do the heart work required to interrupt the barriers that cause them to conform and mask as their Performing Self.
- They are aware of their values and they "walk the talk."

- They are consistent in how they behave regardless of the situation.
- They embrace and showcase their differences even in the face of judgment.
- They share personal details about themselves.
- They speak freely.
- They are genuine in their curiosity to learn about others.
- They get vulnerable.

My work has shown me that an authentic leader is also an inclusive leader. Authentic leaders not only care about understanding, embracing, and sharing their own differences; they also care about encouraging others to know, embrace, and be who they are, including their differences. For example, a leader might share his challenges of juggling parenting with work and he'll show empathy and inquire about other parents' experiences as well.

I will now take you through the following four key strategies for becoming more of an authentic leader:

- Reveal your personal side.
- Create opportunities to share authentically.
- Ask and learn about differences.
- Practice mindful listening.

As I do, consider how you'll leverage these approaches across the range of areas where you lead others.

Reveal Your Personal Side

In our conversation, Kelvin Tran shared with me his belief that "leadership is about being a person." He's bang on. It's so simple, but so often overlooked.

If you want to foster an authentic, inclusive culture and build trust with your team members, then they must see you as more than a representative of the organizational mandate. If all you do is talk about work, not only will you be one of the most boring people on Earth, you'll create tremendous barriers for your team members to talk about anything other than work. They'll constantly be walking on eggshells in your presence because they'll feel the pressure to conform and mask. Instead, you want them to see you as a real person—a complete person—and not just as an organizational automaton.

To be real, don't be afraid to reveal your personal side. By personal side, I'm referring to your history, background, culture, stories, experiences, values, needs, desires, thoughts, feelings, fears, vulnerabilities, and more—*especially* when these areas reflect your differences (let's call this the "personal sharing list"). And I dare you to go even further: share things that connect not only to your professional life but also to who you are outside the doors of your organization (think evenings and weekends). For example, in telling me that he wants his staff to be authentic because "then they'll be the most engaged, happy, and productive," U.S. District Judge Brian C. Wimes noted that to make this happen, "I speak very openly about my own personal and family life, not just my work, because I know that my work life won't get my team to open up."

It's also worth mentioning that sharing what makes you different with your team members will also help you to interrupt minimization—the tendency to focus on commonalities and downplay differences. As a leader, you'll help to create a culture where bringing differences to work is normalized and valued, which are critical aspects for cultivating a more authentic, inclusive, and innovative environment.

I had the pleasure of interviewing Elio Luongo, the CEO of KPMG in Canada. Through our leadership and inclusion work together, I have come to know Elio very well and he has become a dear friend. Elio's remarkable story of success includes working at a gas station when he was fifteen and being raised by Italian immigrant parents. In remembering his deceased father, for whom he has tremendous respect, Elio told me that he learned about the importance of hard work and perseverance by watching his father, who laid pipes on the streets of Vancouver.

From the very first time I met Elio as part of a coaching session I did with him years ago, he has radiated authenticity in our interactions. As I've come to know him, he has repeatedly shared with me his belief that, "even in the face of fear and big risk, being yourself is so key." For Elio, this means trying not to edit his spoken thoughts, and openly sharing about his upbringing (which he refers to as "poor and ambitious") among groups of people who tend to come from an affluent background and among whom Elio has often felt like he doesn't belong.

To become the senior-most leader at KPMG in Canada, Elio had to go through a long selection process, which included an in-person interview with the board of directors. Our interview took place shortly after Elio had taken the helm of the firm, and so I excitedly asked him what took place in the board interview that led him to be selected. He told me, "I had just returned from my vacation in Italy. I was feeling great about myself, about life. I felt really grounded. I went in there and was myself. I was totally real. I talked about my values, my family, about growing up poor and ambitious. I didn't shy away from saying things that I knew might sink me." And when I asked Elio why this was important, he replied, "In being your whole self you signal that you're strong, you're comfortable with you who you are. It lets people know that they can relate to you—because we're the same—vulnerable, afraid, but great."

If this kind of openness about your personal life feels daunting, start small and then go big. Create a "personal sharing list" of things about yourself that you could share in a professional environment but that you're currently not sharing. Then slowly, one by one, start to talk about them at work.

For example, as part of launching my consulting practice after ten years in the legal profession, I vowed to resist the corporate pressure to minimize, by sharing more of myself in my professional interactions. I started by sharing more about being a "Brown girl"—a woman of Punjabi and Sikh heritage—because this is such an integral part of me. I then worked my way up to things that felt like "bigger stakes" to me, such as talking about growing up in an immigrant household and revealing my experiences with racist bullying.

Over the last few years in particular, I've been sharing my insecurities and vulnerabilities in the professional context, which feel like big stakes. For example, I'll tell clients that I'm having a hard time with work and/or life; I'll cry in front of my team (and sometimes even my clients) when I'm feeling overwhelmed or when something personally challenging is happening in my life; and I'll openly admit when I don't know an answer or how to do something. Even here, with "big stakes" sharing, doing it bit by bit makes it easier to be authentic in even more important moments.

I had one of these moments a few years ago with a committee I had just joined. We had met a few times by phone and were still getting to know each other when we met in person for the first time at a conference. I was late for our meeting (as usual)—I came bursting into the room, papers falling out of my hands, feeling really frazzled. After apologizing for being late, I muttered something about being a disheveled mess to the group. One of the committee members responded, "Are you kidding me? You're the most put-together person at this conference—just look at you!"

I instantly knew what she was talking about—what they saw was the image of "she's got her shit together" because I had on a good outfit, I spoke well, and so on. What they couldn't see was that, while on the outside I looked "on point," on the inside I actually was feeling like a mess. In that moment, I had the opportunity to perform or to be real. I said to the group, "Please don't let my packaging fool you. It just hides that I'm feeling really exhausted and unprepared for our meeting." It was amazing how the energy immediately shifted in the room. People started to chime in about feeling the same. It was like watching an ice wall melt.

Sometimes sharing our personal side means advocating for aspects of our identities that are fundamental to who we are (*really* BIG stakes stuff). In our chat, Navdeep Bains, a cabinet minister and Member of Canadian Parliament, told me that as an elected public official he repeatedly has to stand his ground about wearing his *kirpan* while working, when he visits other governments around the world. (The *kirpan* is one of the five Sikh articles of faith. It resembles a knife or sword and, if you choose to wear it, it must not be removed except when bathing. Nav wears a small *kirpan* in a sheath under his clothes). Nav told me that he repeatedly finds himself in highly sensitive, politicized scenarios when security teams will demonstrate some resistance to his article of faith. In these moments, he is either indirectly—or worse yet, directly—asked to remove his *kirpan*. Nav's response? Nope, not gonna do that. He shared that, "while I'm winning small victories, I still feel very nervous and even terrified in moments. But despite this, I still stand my ground."

Sharing your personal side, and especially your differences, will feel awkward for some—perhaps you weren't taught to do this (you were taught to focus on sameness and to minimize); and, in fact, you may have been taught to do the opposite ("Don't talk about personal stuff at work!"). Or perhaps everything from your personal life feels like "big stakes" because you have much self-work to do before you can start sharing. If this is you, I encourage you to practice the strategies outlined in earlier chapters of this book. Start small: reveal something, anything. I promise you that it'll make a difference.

Authentic Leadership Insight
How Much Sharing Is Too Much for a Leader?

In our conversation, Sonya Kunkel, Chief Inclusion Officer and Vice President, People Strategies and Insights at BMO Financial Group, highlighted the challenges a leader may experience in determining just how much of themselves is appropriate to share: "Leaders struggle with showing up authentically, which means being more personal. If it looks hokey, your team will think you're being fake... But you also need to decide your boundaries—what you want to share versus what you don't need to share. You don't want to fall into 'TMI' [too much information], and leave your team with a negative impression. As a leader, you want to find the right balance with what you share and the tone you create."

Sonya is absolutely right. There is such a thing as "oversharing" and, as a leader, you probably don't want to end up there. For each leader, this will be a "use your judgment" experience. You'll want to decide what is the right amount of sharing for your team based on who you are, where your comfort level is with sharing, and what the comfort level of your team members is, among other considerations.

As you develop your authentic leadership muscle by practicing this skill, it will get easier to determine the right level of sharing for you and your team. In the meantime, leverage your emotional intelligence to tune in to how you're feeling as you reveal your personal side and how that information is being received. If your team members demonstrate negative physical signals when you share—for example, exhibiting widened eyes or avoiding eye contact, turning red and splotchy, physically moving away from you, dramatically fidgeting, laughing nervously (or, heaven forbid, a combination of all these things)—you're probably in TMI territory.

Create Opportunities to Share Authentically

In her *Harvard Business Review* article on likeability (co-authored with INSEAD professor Miguel Sousa Lobo), my fellow inclusion advocate, colleague, and an esteemed professor at the University of Toronto's Rotman School of Management, Tiziana Casciaro, notes: "If someone is liked, his colleagues will seek out every little bit of competence he has to offer." Tiziana highlights research that has shown us that we tend to like people we are familiar with (as discussed in chapters 5, 6, and 7), that we like people who have reciprocal positive feelings about us, and that this is even more important than competence.

On how to develop likeability, even among those who are not like us, Tiziana emphasizes the importance of manufacturing liking, which we can do in part by experiencing regular contact with someone, designing processes that give people opportunities to become acquainted and more comfortable with each other, and promoting bonding by putting people through intense, cooperative experiences.[3]

Revealing more of your Authentic Self in impromptu moments when you're not already skilled at doing so may cause you to feel nervous, stressed, or uncomfortable. As soon as you have these feelings, you'll likely end up in fight-or-flight mode (recall your sympathetic nervous system or SNS) and, therefore, you'll be less likely to open up and share. So, as an authentic leader, you can leverage formal opportunities to share more openly and to interact more personally with your team.

I recommend replacing the surface-scratching, two-minute interaction about the weather that you may have with a team member on the elevator, with practices that enable you to share more in-depth personal information at regular intervals. This could happen, for instance, by simply working more closely together (e.g., concentrated time on a project), but it can also happen by collaborating on committees, doing non-profit or charity work, co-authoring a paper, attending a conference, organizing a client or team event, or socializing more often. Because these types of activities require us to spend more time and interact one on one or in small groups, they're ripe for sharing our personal side with one another.

Senator Ratna Omidvar told me that authentic leadership for her is all about sharing meaningful experiences with others. In fact, she said, "The best thing I've ever done to be more authentic is being part of a team of eleven Canadians who sponsored two Syrian refugee families to come to Canada in 2015. The authenticity of this experience is something that I can literally touch and feel."

The point is quite simple: as a leader, it's valuable to be mindful about creating moments when you're being authentic with your team and they feel comfortable reciprocating. If this doesn't come naturally to you, the best way is to establish regular, formal practices or opportunities to encourage personal interaction. It's one of the first steps in replacing systemic minimization with an inclusive culture of authenticity.

Authentic Voices
Check In as a Leader in Meaningful, Structured Ways

Here are a few examples of how leaders I interviewed have created meaningful, structured opportunities for authentic sharing:

Kelvin Tran has created "Popcorn Fridays" in his group. Each Friday, he invites a few team members to get together to share work milestones or successes from the week, while eating popcorn and chatting also about personal things. Kelvin sets the stage by authentically speaking from his own "personal sharing list."

Dr. Catherine Zahn has a practice, after major holidays, of going around the boardroom table and asking her leaders to share what they were most grateful for during the holidays.

Michelle Wimes, Director of Professional Development and Inclusion at Ogletree Deakins P.C., holds regular one-on-one and full-team meetings because, as she puts it, "The more you know and like each other, the better it is and the more likely your team members are to bring their authentic selves to work." At her weekly full-team meetings, Michelle asks each team member to share a moment that they had over the week that surprised or shocked them. She stresses that this type of exploration has been particularly useful for authentic sharing among her team because it starts off the conversation in a personal way.

Stuart Knight, a global leadership speaker and author, suggests that leaders create a "check-in system" to build authenticity into their team interactions. He recommends you start by asking yourself the following questions on a regular basis:
- Once a day: What did I do today that is authentic?
- Once a week: What authentic moments did we have as a team this week?
- Once a month: What activity did the team participate in this month that encouraged authentic moments?

Ask and Learn about Differences

When teaching authenticity and inclusion, I focus on equipping leaders with the tools to ask and learn about differences. What I'm really doing is trying to heighten a leader's ability to

- be more authentic in sharing their own differences,
- encourage their team members to be more authentic in sharing their differences, and
- be aware of their negative judgment of their team members' differences.

Ultimately, I'm teaching leaders to interrupt minimization by focusing on the benefits of understanding and leveraging behavioral differences, rather than pushing behavioral sameness. Recall that when your team members feel like their differences are being ignored or they have to minimize their differences, they are likely to feel excluded and will start to push away from being authentic or adaptive—instead, they'll resort to performing.

In an organizational context, inclusion is about whether your team members feel like they can bring their Authentic Selves—and especially their differences—to work without the fear of adverse consequences. On the flip side, exclusion is about pushing people to conform to the behavior of the dominant culture within the organization by leaving their behavioral differences at the door (a.k.a. minimization). Authenticity is the antidote to exclusion and the key ingredient for building a more inclusive work environment.

It's critical that, as an authentic leader, you signal to your team members that their differences are welcome in your work environment and will be leveraged for everyone's benefit, including that of the organization. To send this message effectively, you must, as their leader, take the initiative to ask and learn about their *differences*. I know from my work how daunting this can be for leaders for whom this is new or uncomfortable territory, but I can't emphasize enough how important this action is in fostering a culture of authenticity.

Here are my best recommendations for how to appropriately ask and learn about a team member's differences:

- **Go there:** Leaders tell me that the main reasons they don't ask about differences are that they don't know how, or they're afraid they'll say something wrong and offend, or they don't want to make someone feel singled out about their differences. I encourage you to interrupt these fears by "going there." In reading this book, you've learned about the benefits of fostering authenticity and you've learned several techniques for making it happen. The more you experience the benefits of doing it, your fears will dissipate. If you're worried about offending someone or getting in trouble with your human resources department (or the law), use your judgment. Generally speaking, when a team member voluntarily shares a difference with you, you're probably fine.

- **Follow this two-part formula:** The easiest place to start is by latching on to the differences that people share with you voluntarily, instead of probing to uncover what is distinctive about them. To overcome your discomfort here, use my tried/tested/true formula for asking about differences. This formula has two parts (and if you'd like to hear me talk more about this, you can Google my Walrus Talk to watch it on YouTube):

  - First, say something to the effect of, "I don't know a lot about X. Can I please ask you about it?" Replace X with whatever the difference is (growing up on a farm, practicing Islam, using a wheelchair, following electronic dance music, etc.). Note that you must include the "Can I please ask you about X?" because you need the team member's permission to "go there." Sometimes the voices of difference don't want to share.

- Second, say something to the effect of "I really want to learn, so I'm sorry in advance if I say something wrong." Why do you say this? Because (1) when we ask about something we know little or nothing about, we're bound to say something wrong at some point, so I think it makes it easier on the receiving end when a person knows that you may not get it right when you're asking; and (2) it signals positive intent—that you're not being a jerk in asking, and that you actually want to learn.

Authentic Leadership Insight
Be Authentic About Difficult Issues

I have repeatedly found myself in the following situation: I'm in a corporate boardroom to teach inclusion and the only person of color in the room will courageously share how difficult it has felt to come into work during the days following another police killing of an unarmed Black man or after another White supremacist has attacked a house of worship, and no one in the office speaks about the killings despite the massive media coverage and the impact. In the face of "It's business as usual at ABC Corp," the person of color will share that they self-silence about how they're hurting; they put on a happy face and act like everything is great; and they chime in about whatever the hot topics are in the office banter that day (like last night's ball game).

After the person of color shares their feelings, inevitably White people in the room (most often the leaders) will reveal that they, too, have wanted to talk about how upset they've been feeling and to ask team members about how they're doing, but they haven't for two primary reasons: (1), they're not sure if it's okay to talk about this at work; and, (2), they don't know how to bring it up.

I empathize with both the person of color and the White leaders in the room. I know firsthand what it's like to self-silence and hide the pain that ties back to racism. But I also know what it's like to self-silence as a leader—I used to hold back in asking people in the workplace about how they're feeling about a social issue because I wasn't sure if it was appropriate to do so and I definitely didn't want to offend. This was until I came to see the benefits of "going there" with difficult conversations.

To be an authentic and inclusive leader, it's crucial that you talk about what's happening in society—if we're giving airtime to sports events, we must make room for expression about social issues and world events. The way to do this is to just bring it up. For example, to the question "How are you doing?" you can respond truthfully and say something like "To be candid, I'm quite upset. I couldn't sleep last night after watching the news about another police killing. Did you watch the coverage?"

If you're going to be the change as a leader, it means changing how you behave. And this is how you do it.

Practice Mindful Listening

Several of the people I interviewed emphasized the importance of listening in order to be an authentic leader—listening both to oneself and to others. For example, Seema Jethalal, an arts community leader and activist, told me that she practices "deep listening" as an authentic leader, a concept that was inspired by Indigenous elder Duke Redbird. Seema describes deep listening as "talking less, listening more, asking open-ended questions without judgment, and using a casual tone and relaxed body language." She said, "This enables me to be disarming and to develop trusting rapports, which in turn, encourages the people I'm speaking with to be more authentic with me."

We've explored the concept of listening to oneself—identifying who you are, what is getting in the way of being yourself, and how to leverage strategies that resonate with you in order to practice being yourself consistently. To accomplish all of this, you need to tune in to yourself so that you can hear your own thoughts and feelings, which will tell you exactly what you need to do. But in order to be an authentic leader, it's also critical that you develop excellent listening abilities for when others are speaking to you.

With this in mind, there are three types of listening we'll now explore:

1   Self-focused listening—puts a spotlight on you
2   Two-way listening—focuses on the other person
3   Mindful listening—absorbs information from all directions

With self-focused listening, you're anchored to preparing your response to what your team member is saying, rather than actually listening to what the person is saying. Picture the following going on in your head: "Umm, I can't believe Kiran just said X. Has he not been hearing what I've been saying over the last month at our performance review meetings? I'm going to remind him about what I told him. But when will he stop talking?! Whatever, I'm going to interrupt him." (Many of us, most of the time?)

With two-way listening, you're focused on your team member—you're paying attention to his words and his body language. But you're also tuned in to what you're thinking and feeling. Picture the following going on in your head: "Hmm, Kiran just said he agrees, but his body language makes me feel like he's only saying it. I wonder if he's saying it just to make me happy? Especially considering I remember him saying something different last month. I don't feel good about this; it's making me feel uncomfortable. Should I ask him about what he really thinks? Maybe I shouldn't. Or maybe I should? Hmm, I'm gonna leave it—we don't have enough time." (Some of us, some of the time?)

With mindful listening, you're taking in everything around you—paying attention to what your team member is saying, his body language, the energy he's emitting, the feelings and body sensations you're having, the thoughts in your head, and what's happening in the environment around you. Picture the following going on in your head: "Kiran seems to be off today—he hasn't spoken throughout this team meeting and he's hunched over in his chair. Hmm, I wonder if it has something to do with the fact that he's the most junior in the room? In fact, now that I'm paying more attention, it seems that only the extroverted leaders are speaking. The introverts aren't sharing at all. And I'm sure most of us don't even agree with the loud voices. *I'm* not even feeling that comfortable as a leader in this room. I'm going to interrupt the conversation to share my dissenting views, then I'm going to ask for the voices who haven't been heard about their thoughts, including Kiran's." (Very few of us, and rarely?)

I love the concept of mindful listening. In taking in everything around you, you'll focus on tuning in to your team members' needs, your needs, and the needs of others who are present. All of this will help you to be more tuned in to being present, focused, and deliberate in being authentic, which of course will help you to create the container for others to be more authentic themselves.

To get into the right mindset for mindful listening, you'll want to leverage several of the strategies outlined in earlier chapters:

- Engage in self-reflection practices.
- Understand your Authentic Self.
- Identify the barriers that cause you to conform and mask.

- Maintain a mindfulness practice.
- Challenge and replace your negative narratives.
- Use body postures to change how you're feeling.
- Practice self-care of your body and mind.

To actually engage in mindful listening, here are a few practical suggestions to help you:

- **Pay attention to your breath:** Ensure that you're engaging in diaphragm breathing (see the description on how to do this in chapter 9). This technique will cause you to relax both mentally and physically, and allow you to better hear your thoughts and feel the sensations in your body and be more aware of the environment you're in.

- **Tune in to how you're feeling in the moment:** What physical sensations are you feeling in your body and what do they mean? What thoughts are dancing in your head while the person is sharing? What is happening in the environment that is impacting your experience? Is anything triggering you to perform?

- **Tune in to the other person:** Listen to their words (what are they saying?), pay attention to their body language (what non-verbal signals are they giving you?), and take notice of whether there's a disconnect between what they're saying and how they're emoting or what their body language is communicating. Could anything you're doing be triggering them to perform?

- **Take in the environment with your senses:** What's happening in the room? Is anything happening that could be impacting how the person is sharing or how you're receiving what the person is sharing? What might be happening that's making it harder for you to be authentic or for the other person to be authentic?

- **Take your time:** Give the person you're with the time and space to articulate what they want to say, and then give yourself time and space to do the same. You will offer a more genuine, authentic response to what they are actually expressing if you listen in this manner.

Now let's take a moment to pause so you can reflect on the insights and strategies shared in this chapter, in order to help you develop and hone your authentic leadership skills going forward.

Reflection Moment

- In what ways are you privileged, and how do your forms of privilege enable you to live, work, and lead more authentically?

- Are there areas in your interactions where you expect team members to conform or mask who they are? In which of the Seven Behavioral Dimensions *(described in detail on pages 23-24)* is this happening? Why?

- What specific things are you currently not sharing at work, and what would you be comfortable revealing from your "personal sharing list" (your history, background, culture, stories, experiences, values, needs, desires, thoughts, feelings, fears, insecurities, etc.) going forward?

- What do you already know about each team member from their "personal sharing list," and what will you start to ask about going forward?

- What structured opportunities will you create to share with your team members after today?

- How will you ask and learn about differences among your team members going forward?

- How will you practice mindful listening after today?

AUTHENTIC LEADERS believe in the transformative power of the Authenticity Principle because they know it will enable them to

- increasingly bring more of their Authentic Self to work;
- help others within the organization be more of themselves;
- signal that differences are valued;
- leverage their own and others' differences;
- create a culture where being authentic is normalized;
- contribute to enhancing key talent management areas;
- enhance creativity, innovation, and the bottom line; and
- make their workplace a more fun vibrant place to be.

They know there's a huge payoff—personal, professional, and organizational—for nurturing an authentic, inclusive organizational culture. Like my friend Elio, authentic leaders courageously walk the talk in how they live, work, and lead despite the fear of judgment and despite experiencing the push to conform themselves. They're trailblazers, keen to bring about change within their organizations, and so they take action to make it happen.

Have the courage, the audacity, the vision to *be* an authentic leader.

Conclusion
The Authenticity Revolution

My life amounts to no more than one drop in a limitless ocean.
Yet what is any ocean, but a multitude of drops?

DAVID MITCHELL, *CLOUD ATLAS*

Y EARS AGO, upon finishing my yoga teacher training in India during the work sabbatical I mentioned previously, I returned with a commitment to honor my true self and my values in how I was choosing to behave. I was back working in the corporate world at the same fancy law firm job, so I was still exploring what this commitment meant for me. What I did know is that I needed to live, work, and lead with more of an authentic spirit.

Shortly after I returned, I attended a karaoke social event for the lawyers at my firm. I went even though I didn't want to—I tend to dislike karaoke because I rarely know and like the music on offer (it's usually a combo of bad '80s rock and '90s pop). I was standing with a small group of people—mostly junior lawyers, one senior partner/leader, and me wearing my management hat—looking at the list of songs for an option that we could sing together.

It was proving to be quite a challenge. The leader was naming song after song and, while a few others were giving their approval, I kept responding with some variation of "Umm, I don't know that one." I had a moment of wondering if I ought to just say, "Great, let's do that one!" and then pretend to sing along or hide in the bathroom.

The leader finally turned to me and said in an animated voice, "What, did you grow up under a rock?!" The group broke out into laughter.

My cheeks started to burn as it took me back to childhood experiences of being laughed at, and for a second I wished I could evaporate. But something deep within took ahold of me, and instead of remaining silent, I responded with both humor and sass, "Nope, I didn't grow up under a rock! I grew up in a household listening to Bollywood and bhangra music—do they have any of that?" Some people in the group smiled, and the leader glanced at me with an "Ohhh, right" look on his face. Handing me the song sheet, he then asked, "What song works for you?" I felt myself not only relax but I also felt a surge of confidence.

Then a junior lawyer of East Asian descent gently turned to me and whispered, "I thought I was the only one who didn't know any of these songs! I grew up listening to K-pop [Korean pop]."

I smiled and said, "Let's choose one together," and handed her the song sheet.

This is exactly what the Authenticity Principle is about: choosing to be more of who you are, especially what makes you different, so that you can leverage your empowerment to help others do the same. And this is particularly important when, in your capacity as a lover, parent, sibling, friend, teacher, leader, and more, you have greater social and personal power to do this. By bringing this spirit to your interactions, you help to celebrate differences and build a shared experience of openness, belonging, and acceptance—something that we desperately need as individuals and as a society.

A REVOLUTION is about overthrowing a current system for a new system. My foremost wish is that the Authenticity Principle ignites a revolution.

Our society needs a new paradigm for how we treat each other based on our differences. Our failure to understand, appreciate, and leverage each other's differences is causing us to suffer. From the pressure to conform to the constant fear of judgment, many of us suffer in silence because we feel marginalized, and yet we're part of a larger community that is hurting.

I'm advocating for the Authenticity Principle to become a new way of understanding the interconnectedness of being—in other words, you are not alone. Your struggle is part of the larger human struggle, the same way that your experiences of joy and love are part of the larger human experience. Instead of fearing, judging, and minimizing our own and others' differences, we must work together to interrupt our personal and societal ways of being in order to address the negative repercussions of our intolerance.

I'm calling on you to change your mindset *and* your actions by using authenticity. To quote the prolific African-American spoken-word poet and musician Gil Scott-Heron, "The revolution will not be televised [nor in this era will it be online] . . . The revolution will be live." Anchor to your imperative for being more authentic and then take action in order to live, work, and lead in alignment—not just for yourself, but for the betterment of our society as we seek to collectively heal and thrive.

Choose to know, embrace, and be who you are. Share your differences and what makes you unique. As much as possible. Start now.

Endnotes

Chapter 1: A New Way of Understanding Authenticity (page 12)

1 Brown, Brené. *The Gifts of Imperfection: Let Go of Who You Think You're Supposed to Be and Embrace Who You Are* (Center City, MN: Hazelden, 2010).
Brown, Brené. "My response to Adam Grant's New York Times Op/ED: Unless You're Oprah, 'Be Yourself' Is Terrible Advice," *LinkedIn,* June 5, 2016. (www.linkedin.com/pulse/my-response-adam-grants-new-york-times-oped-unless-youre-bren%C3%A9-brown)
Pasricha, Neil. "The 3 A's of awesome," TEDxToronto transcript, September 2010. (https://www.ted.com/talks/neil_pasricha_the_3_a_s_of_awesome/transcript?language=en)

2 Kernis, Michael H. and Brian M. Goldman. "A Multicomponent Conceptualization of Authenticity: Theory and Research," *Advances in Experimental Social Psychology* 38 (2006): 283-357, doi: 10.1016/S0065-2601(06)38006-9.
Goldman, Brian Middleton and Michael H. Kernis. "The Role of Authenticity in Healthy Psychological Functioning and Subjective Well-Being," *Annals of the American Psychotherapy Association* 5, no. 6 (2002): 18-20.
Seligman, Martin E. P. et. al. "Positive Psychology Progress: Empirical Validation of Interventions," *American Psychologist* 60, no. 5 (2005): 410-421, doi: 10.1037/0003-066X.60.5.410.

3 Curtin, Melanie. "This 75-Year Harvard Study Found the 1 Secret to Leading a Fulfilling Life," *Inc.*, February 27, 2017. (www.inc.com/melanie-curtin/want-a-life-of-fulfillment-a-75-year-harvard-study-says-to-prioritize-this-one-t.html)

4 Lyubomirsky, Sonja, Laura King and Ed Diener. "The Benefits of Frequent Positive Affect: Does Happiness Lead to Success?", *Psychological Bulletin* 131, no. 6 (2005): 823, doi: 10.1037/0033-2909.131.6.803.
Achor, Shawn. *The Happiness Advantage: The Seven Principles of Positive Psychology that Fuel Success and Performance at Work* (New York: Crown Business, 2010).

5 Cuddy, Amy. *Presence: Bringing Your Boldest Self to Your Biggest Challenges* (New York: Little, Brown and Company, 2015), 36.

Chapter 2: Your Authentic Self (page 29)

1   Walton, Mark. "Why We're Hardwired for Midlife Reinvention," Next Avenue, November 19, 2012. (www.nextavenue.org/ why-were-hardwired-midlife-reinvention-and-boundless-potential/) Strauch, Barbara; interview by Tara Parker-Pope. "The Talents of a Middle-Aged Brain," Well (blog), *New York Times,* April 30, 2010. (well.blogs.nytimes. com/2010/04/30/the-talents-of-a-middle-aged-brain/)

2   Thomas Fuller (1654–1734).

Chapter 4: Your Performing Self (page 56)

1   Brown, Brené. *The Gifts of Imperfection: Let Go of Who You Think You're Supposed to Be and Embrace Who You Are* (Center City, MN: Hazelden, 2010), 25–26.

Chapter 5: What Triggers You to Perform? (page 68)

1   Goffman, Erving. *Stigma: Notes on the Management of Spoiled Identity* (New York: Simon & Schuster, 1963), 102.

2   Yoshino, Kenji. *Covering: The Hidden Assault on Our Civil Rights* (New York: Random House, 2006). Yoshino, Kenji and Christie Smith. "Uncovering talent: A new model of inclusion," Deloitte University Leadership Center for Inclusion, December 6, 2013. (www2.deloitte.com/content/dam/Deloitte/us/Documents/about-deloitte/us-inclusion-uncovering-talent-paper.pdf)

3   Ruiz, Don Miguel. *The Four Agreements: A Practical Guide to Personal Freedom* (San Rafael, CA: Amber-Allen Publishing, 1997), 6–9.

4   Grant, Adam. *Originals: How Non-Conformists Move the World* (New York: Viking, 2016), 163, 168–169.

5   Bradshaw, Catherine P., Anne L. Sawyer and Lindsey M. O'Brennan. "Bullying and peer victimization at school: perceptual differences between students and school staff," *School Psychology Review* 26, no. 3 (2007): 361–382.

6   Coughlan, Sean. "Childhood bullying 'damages adult life'," BBC News, August 19, 2013. (www.bbc.com/news/education-23756749)

Chapter 6: The Workplace Is the Adult Sandbox for Performing (page 86)

1   Minimization highlights commonalities in basic human needs and values that can mask a deeper understanding of cultural differences: "Minimization can take one of two forms: (a) the highlighting of commonalities due to limited cultural self-understanding, which is more commonly experienced by dominant group members within a cultural community; or (b) the highlighting of commonalities as a strategy for navigating the values and practices largely determined by the dominant culture group, which is more often experienced by non-dominant group members within a larger cultural community." "Intercultural Development Continuum," Intercultural Development Inventory, accessed January 16, 2017. (idiinventory.com/ products/the-intercultural-development-continuum-idc/)

2 Hammer, Mitchell R., Milton J. Bennett and Richard Wiseman. "Measuring intercultural sensitivity: The intercultural development inventory," *International Journal of Intercultural Relations* 27, no. 4 (July 2003): 421–443, doi: 10.1016/S0147-1767(03)00032-4.
The IDI is grounded in the Intercultural Development Continuum, a research-based adaptation of the Developmental Model of Intercultural Sensitivity originally proposed by Dr. Milton Bennett. The IDI assesses intercultural competence in terms of six developmental orientations: Denial, Polarization, Minimization, Acceptance, and Adaptation (see www.idiinventory.com).

3 The IDI results follow a normal distribution, and so approximately 68 percent of the general population will fall within Minimization. This is why the overwhelming majority of people who have taken the IDI are in Minimization and why the overwhelming majority of organizations are in Minimization. Spencer, Steven J, Christine Logel, and Paul G. Davies. "Stereotype Threat," Annual Review of Psychology 67 (2016): 415–437, doi: 10.1146/annurev-psych-073115-103235.

4 Yoshino, Kenji and Christie Smith. "Uncovering talent: A new model of inclusion," Deloitte University Leadership Center for Inclusion, December 6, 2013. (www2.deloitte.com/content/dam/Deloitte/us/Documents/about-deloitte/us-inclusion-uncovering-talent-paper.pdf)

Chapter 7: Embrace Who You Are and Stop Performing (page 99)

1 Neff, Kristen. "Definition of Self-Compassion," Self Compassion, accessed January 16, 2017. (self-compassion.org/the-three-elements-of-self-compassion-2/)

2 "Skin-tone," Project Implicit, accessed January 16, 2017. (implicit.harvard.edu/implicit/canada/background/skininfo.html)

3 McKenzie, Kwame. "Racism and health: Antiracism is an important health issue," *BMJ* 326, no. 7380 (January 2003): 65–66. (www.ncbi.nlm.nih.gov/pmc/articles/PMC1125019/)
Silverstein, Jason. "How Racism Is Bad for Our Bodies," *The Atlantic*, March 12, 2013. (www.theatlantic.com/health/archive/2013/03/how-racism-is-bad-for-our-bodies/273911/)

4 Project Implicit, accessed January 16, 2017. (implicit.harvard.edu/)

5 Banaji, Mahzarin R. and Anthony G. Greenwald. *Blind Spot: Hidden Biases of Good People* (New York: Random House, 2013), 115.

6 "FAQs," Project Implicit, accessed January 16, 2017. (implicit.harvard.edu/implicit/demo/background/faqs.html#faq19)

7 The full test is available on Dr. Clance's website (www.paulineroseclance.com). Clance, Pauline Rose. *The Impostor Phenomenon: When Success Makes You Feel Like a Fake* (Toronto: Bantam Books, 1985), 20–22.

8 Cuddy, Amy. *Presence: Bringing Your Boldest Self to Your Biggest Challenges* (New York: Little, Brown and Company, 2015), 94.

9   Wegner, Daniel M. "Ironic Processes of Mental Control," *Psychological Review* 101, no. 1 (1994): 34-52, doi: 10.1037/0033-295X.101.1.34.

10 Dr. Jill Bolte Taylor's website, accessed January 16, 2016. (drjilltaylor.com/about.html)

11 Taylor, Jill Bolte. *My Stroke of Insight: A Brain Scientist's Personal Journey* (New York: Viking, 2008), 153.

Chapter 8: Your Adapted Self (page 123)

1   Cain, Susan. *Quiet: The Power of Introverts in a World That Can't Stop Talking* (New York: Crown Publishers, 2012), 210.

Chapter 9: Practice Being Authentic and Adaptive (page 134)

1   While widely attributed to Anaïs Nin, the origin of this quote is disputed.

2   Dweck, Carol. *Mindset: The New Psychology of Success* (New York: Ballantine Books, 2006).

3   Adams, Linda. "Learning a New Skill Is Easier Said Than Done," Gordon Training International, accessed January 14, 2017. (www.gordontraining.com/free-workplace-articles/learning-a-new-skill-is-easier-said-than-done/)

4   Hanson, Rick. *Buddha's Brain: The Practical Neuroscience of Happiness, Love, and Wisdom* (Oakland, CA: New Harbinger Publications, 2009), 3-4 and 72. Goleman, Daniel. "Developing emotional intelligence," April 3, 2013. (www.danielgoleman.info/developing-emotional-intelligence/)

5   Hanson, Rick. *Buddha's Brain: The Practical Neuroscience of Happiness, Love, and Wisdom* (Oakland, CA: New Harbinger Publications, 2009), 73.

6   Cuddy, Amy. *Presence: Bringing Your Boldest Self to Your Biggest Challenges* (New York: Little, Brown and Company, 2015), 255-256.

7   Cuddy, Amy. *Presence: Bringing Your Boldest Self to Your Biggest Challenges* (New York: Little, Brown and Company, 2015), 241.

8   Hanson, Rick. *Buddha's Brain: The Practical Neuroscience of Happiness, Love, and Wisdom* (Oakland, CA: New Harbinger Publications, 2009), 80-86.

Chapter 10: Leaders, Be the Change (page 155)

1   Gardner, William L. et al. "'Can you see the real me?' A self-based model of authentic leader and follower development," *The Leadership Quarterly* 16, (2005): 343-372.
    Hassan, Arif and Forbis Ahmed. "Authentic Leadership, Trust and Work Engagement," *International Journal of Social, Behavioral, Educational, Economic, Business and Industrial Engineering* 5, no. 8 (2011): 1036-1042.
    Menard, Julie and Luc Brunet. "Authenticity and well-being in the workplace: a mediation model," *Journal of Managerial Psychology* 26, no. 4 (2011): 331-346.
    Wang, D., and C. Hsieh. "The Effect of Authentic Leadership on Employee Trust and Employee Engagement," *Social Behavior and Personality: An International Journal* 41, (2013): 613-624.

2   Hunt, Vivian, Dennis Layton and Sara Prince. "Diversity Matters" McKinsey & Company, February 2, 2015. (www.mckinsey.com/~/media/mckinsey/business functions/organization/our insights/why diversity matters/diversity matters. ashx)
Page, Scott E. *The Difference: How the Power of Diversity Creates Better Groups, Firms, Schools, and Societies* (Woodstock: Princeton University Press, 2007).
3   Casciaro, Tiziana and Miguel Sousa Lobo. "Competent Jerks, Lovable Fools, and the Formation of Social Networks," *Harvard Business Review,* June 2005. (hbr.org/2005/06/ competent-jerks-lovable-fools-and-the-formation-of-social-networks)

Acknowledgements (a.k.a. "Props" and "Fist Bumps")

IF LIVING authentically is transformative, so is writing a book about it. Writing this book has changed my life.

Before I started the journey, I reached out to friends and colleagues who are authors, to get their guidance on what the process would be like, and they were so right: writing a book is really hard work and it will kick your ass, but you will be better for it. And I am.

I would not have been able to write this book without an army of people who helped me to brainstorm, research, shape, and manage the process along the way. But I also would not have been able to create this book without the guidance, wisdom, support, and love of truckloads of people who helped me to get to a place where I would have something valuable to write about. So my thank-you's go out to many for helping me to get to this place.

Please prepare yourself for an epic soliloquy of love.

To my kick-ass team at bhasin consulting inc. (bci), thank you for working so hard on our mission, for doing your best in all that you do, and for helping me to shine. I will never tire of saying that I would not be able to do what I do without your support. I'm so grateful. I'd like to thank all my past and present bci team members who have helped with the book and more: Sarah Israel, Alyse Runyan, Natasha Patel, Anitra Steinberg, Winston Gee, Amrit Dhillon, Brian Lynch, Maria Rivera, Vanessa Lucchetta, Shayna Mistry, Joanna Kirke, Coralie D'Souza, and Kate Julien. I want to give a very special thanks to Stephanie Damgaard, who has been my "go to" rock and the voice of reason throughout the book-writing process—you are so talented and I'm eternally thankful for all you have done to support my book and me (every time I don a red dress or see a blue cover, I will think of you!).

To my awesome team at Page Two Strategies, thank you for your hard work throughout this process. You constantly showed up when we needed you and I'm so grateful for your direction, insight, and efforts. I'd like to thank my editing team, Karen Milner, Lindsay Humphreys, and especially Amanda Lewis (you rock) for their hard work, and the rest of my Page Two team: Gabrielle Narsted, Megan Jones, Peter Cocking, Zoe Grams, and Erin Parker. And, of course, to the captain of the Page Two ship, Jesse Finkelstein: You are so incredibly kind, generous, and professional. Thank you for believing in my message and believing in me. I felt your warmth and support all along this process.

To all the incredible people who agreed to be interviewed, who read drafts of the manuscript, who helped to thrash out ideas and concepts, and who gave me advice along the way, a *huge* thank you. I would not have been able to write this book without our invaluable conversations and your contributions. Thank you to: Alex Kopelman, Annahid Dashtgard, Brian C. Wimes, Brigid Dineen, Bruce Croxon, Caroline Abela (twenty-three years!), Dr. Catherine Zahn, Charles Lee, Che Kothari, Chris Miller, Cristina Bonini, Deepa Mehta, Deland Kamanga, Donald Guloien, Drew Dudley, Catherine Riddell, Cinnie Noble, Craig Strong (thank you for always keepin' it real), Dr. Eddie Moore Jr., Erica Young (my sista!), Gabrielle Scrimshaw, Gunjan Goel, Heanda Radomski, Heidi Levine, Ivy Wong, Jai-Jagdeesh (for your music and our interview), Jim Fisher, Jim Leipold, Joyce Roche, Karlyn

Percil-Mercieca, Kate Hilton, Kelvin Tran, Kenji Yoshino, Kristine Remedios, Kristy Carscallen, Leah Eichler, Lori Lorenzo, Lori Simpson, Mary Lou Maher, Michael Bungay Stanier, Michelle Grocholsky, Michelle Wimes, Dr. Mitchell Hammer, Navdeep Bains, Nicole Chrolavicius (my Partinaire until the end of time), Nicole Phillips (girl, your help during this time was invaluable!), Pamela Palmater, Pauleanna Reid, Prubjoth Sidhu, Ramandeep Grewal (I adore ya, big sis), Senator Ratna Omidvar, Reva Seth, Reza Satchu, Richard Meade, Rob Granatstein, Sang Lee, Savaria Harris, Sean Bailey, Sean Tompkins, Seema Jethalal, Shakil Choudhury, Sonya Kunkel, Stuart Knight, Tim Leishman, Tim Thompson, and Verna Myers (sista soulja, love you!).

To all my mentors, sponsors, champions, clients, and dear friends whose support throughout my career positioned me to write a book in the first place, thank you for your light. Thank you to: the three people who believed in me right from the launch of bci—Laleh Moshiri, Janet Hoyt, and Joanne Clarfield Schaefer; Ed Babin, who mentored me over fifteen years ago and then put a roof over bci's head for years (which has meant more to me than you'll ever know); Josée Bouchard; Anne Ristic; Nouman Ashraf, for pushing me to do my MBA; Allison Quennell; the CAUFP community; Sonia Menon; the formidable KPMG Canada team (Kristine Remedios, Mary Lou Maher, Bill Thomas, Kim Brewer, and, of course, Elio Luongo); Amy Hanen, Debbie Lachmansingh, Kelvin Tran, and the rest of the teams at TD Bank and Ascend; Charlotte Wager; Jami de Lou; Melique Jones; Mary Schaus; Amandeep Sidhu; Brent Hawkins; Mary Jackson; Deborah Glatter; Jennifer Zephirin; Melinda Marshall; Danyale Price; Renauld Clarke; Jennifer Reynolds; Denise O'Neil-Green; Dr. Mohamed Lachemi; Bindu Dhaliwal; Kathleen Hogan; Ray Adlington; David Komlos; Tiska Wiedermann; Tim Cork; Brian Finlay, Frank Walwyn, Greg Richards, and Raj Anand (my WeirFoulds LLP mentors); Charlie Coffey; Andy Barrie, Matt Galloway, Morgan Passi, and Nick Davis of CBC Radio; the Hazelton

Group (go women of color!); my Mastermind group at Verity (sorry for being so AWOL), and my girls Kori Carew, Genhi Bailey, Maja Hazell, and Manar Morales (y'all are so special to me).

To all the special teachers I had along my journey of learning as a child and as an adult, thank you for helping to give me wind for my sails. Thank you to: my grade three teacher, Mrs. Maclean; my grade six teachers, Mr. Taylor, Mr. Mitanoff, and Mrs. Murphy; my finite math teacher, Mr. Smith (I'll never forget when you told me I would do something special one day); my high school English teacher, Mrs. Kostandoff; my law school professors, Bob Solomon, Ian Kerr, and Nathalie Des Rosiers; and my MBA professors, Ajay Agrawal, Dr. Beatrix Dart, and Rick Powers (a special thank you, Rick, for demonstrating how a sponsor can show up for you).

To the village that it takes to run my life, thank you for keeping me together during these last two years. Thank you to: my brotha, Ali "The Answer" Rahnamoon; my darling Pri (baby sis!); Jane Sloan; Kay Ann Ward; Csilla; Hana; Brooke Pancer; Judy Lawrence; Shant Iskander; Sonya Schaefer; and the Verity team, especially Angela, for being so nice to me during the days I slogged away at book writing.

To the musical geniuses who are my salvation during tough—and joyful—times, thank you. In particular, to Snatam Kaur and DJ Private Ryan (I wasn't kidding; I'm your number-one fan), you have no idea how much you've helped to lift me along the way.

To my beloved angels, who are the reason I breathe, words will never be able to capture my gratitude for your love during this time (when you most certainly didn't get the best of me!). In particular, thank you to my sister, Komal Bhasin, who is my favorite person in the whole wide world (SAGG, GOL, and BTT!), and to my parents, Avinash and Mohanjit Bhasin, for being there for me and for giving me life. Thank you to my adorb nieces, Mya and Simmi (I repeatedly watched your videos to cheer me up on dark days), and my bro-in-law, Sumit Bhatia. And to the rest of my "peeps" who cheered me on, who motivated me, who partied with me, who cried with me (cuz there were lots of tears, as ya know), and who kept me strong, I'm sending y'all so much love: the Dhillons (Neenu, Sonny, Sohina, Harmeena, and Kushal); my Bindra sisters (Ameesha, Arvin, Jessica, and Priyanka); Rita (RD!) and Surinder Dhillon; the "Lovely Liangs" (Mama Maria, Papa Tom, and my sis, Rachel); Ricco and Raman Bhasin; TKLL; the Fourstas; Rishi Kataria, Anjalee Nagrecha, and Neeraj Seth; Allen and Tatanya Benjamin and Del Miller; Mike Silverberg (twenty-seven years!), my B-Girlz Crew (GG, Leezy, Priya, Mandy, Naz, Dee, and Fizza); Kiisha Morrow and Rebecca Wollensack; Patrick Campbell; Sheika Hecker; Clare Ellis; Aime Bwakira and Gwashali Shivute; the Sparks (I love you all—you make me so proud!); Marilyn Chambers; Monique Johnson; and Silas Yamey.

Lastly, I want to express my thanks to the Divine. *Sabna Jiya Ka Ek Data So Mai Visar Na Jaye* — Japji Sahib, Sri Guru Granth Sahib.

[MIC DROP.]

About Ritu Bhasin, LL.B., MBA

RITU BHASIN didn't always feel empowered to be an unapologetic, fiercely authentic leader. While she was highly successful and living the "corporate dream" in her early career, Ritu had a startling realization: the person she was in her day-to-day life bore little resemblance to her true self. Because of her experiences with racism and bullying, she found herself minimizing racial, religious, gender, and class-based aspects of her identity to "fit in" among circles where she felt she didn't belong. And in doing this, she was profoundly unhappy.

After much soul-searching, Ritu decided to transform her life. She completed her MBA, left her corporate job, launched her own business, became a mindfulness practitioner and teacher, and dedicated her life to helping others become more empowered and inclusive. Most importantly, she committed to living as authentically as possible in all that she did going forward.

In 2010, Ritu launched bhasin consulting inc., a diversity and inclusion-focused consulting firm, and has since gained a global reputation for her work in leadership development, diversity and inclusion, and women's advancement. Through her work, Ritu is committed to disrupting the status quo to build a world in which each of us celebrates our own differences and the differences of others. She has delivered talks to thousands, inspiring leaders to be more inclusive, and encouraging those who have experienced oppression to be more empowered. Ritu has won numerous awards for her work, including the City of Toronto's William P. Hubbard Award for Race Relations.

Ritu lives in Toronto, Canada, but travels all over the world to eat, swim, hike, dance, and work.

ritubhasin.com

Visit and subscribe for bonus content,
resources, special offers, and more.